the SODA FOUNTAIN

the SODA FOUNTAIN

FLOATS, SUNDAES, EGG CREAMS & MORE—
Flavors and Traditions of an American Original

GIA GIASULLO AND PETER FREEMAN

with Elizabeth Kiem *and* Nelle Gretzinger

Photography by Michael Harlan Turkell

Ten Speed Press

Berkeley

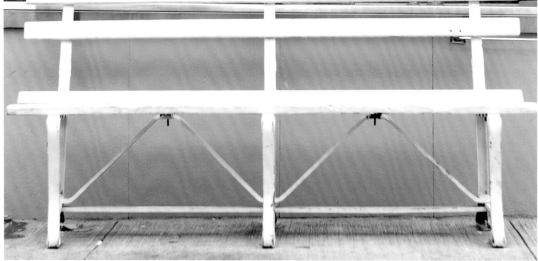

CONTENTS

FROM OUR COUNTER TO YOURS

We didn't invent the soda fountain; we just welcomed it into the twenty-first century with love and reverence.

When Brooklyn Farmacy & Soda Fountain opened its doors in the summer of 2010, our lines were out the door. Almost a century after the fountain's glory days, it appeared that folks were still thirsty for those countertop classics—the sundae, the soda, and the ice cream float.

Our customers came from down the street, from out of town, and sometimes straight from the airport. And the busier we got, the clearer it became that we had not opened a new place. We had opened an old place.

The soda fountain reigned supreme for over one hundred years, touching the lives of three generations of Americans. We know this because we meet people every day who stop in for more than an afternoon treat. They visit because their grandfather owned a pharmacy, their uncle was a "soda jerk," or their parents' first kiss was over a shared malt. They recognize the counter as the place where the Depression was easier to endure and Main Street was more fun. More importantly, they see a place where socializing is done in real time and where kids are more engrossed in our counter than in their electronic devices. They know a good tradition when they see one.

We suspect that you might be holding this book for the same reason. So here is our contribution to a great American tradition: a slice of history with double scoop of how-to.

We hope it hits the spot.

GIA GIASULLO & PETER FREEMAN

CHAPTER ONE

THE SODA FOUNTAIN COMES FROM Rx

There's a reason why our place is called Brooklyn Farmacy and not "Pete's Treats" or "Gia's Gelato" or something equally wholesome and seductive to a sweet tooth. Before we arrived, the storefront on the corner of Henry and Sackett Streets was, in fact, a pharmacy.

Longo's Pharmacy served the neighborhood for more than half a century before it closed in 1969, amid investigations of alleged gun smuggling. That's a story specific to our storefront, and only slightly less sordid than it sounds. The bigger story—the one shared by every American soda fountain that's ever served up a phosphate or a float—is not about firearms; it's about customer service, quality control, and drugs.

Drugs?

Well, yes.

Before it became a spigot of sweet cream and sarsaparilla, the American soda fountain served as a dispenser of health. Soda water was first recognized as a medicinal draught—a natural tonic that eased dyspepsia, nerves, fatigue, and more. The fact that it mixed easily with medicinal tinctures and improved their bitter taste made fizzy water all the more attractive to the apothecaries who served as Main Street's family physicians. Two hundred years ago, soda water was the aspirin of its day. And a profitable one at that.

We know you feel better after an ice cream soda. Feeling good (and sometimes really, really good) has *always* been the objective of the soda fountain. At the pharmacy, where mind- and mood-altering substances were plentiful, the ingredients for health and happiness were passed easily over the counter. A century ago, more often than not, that counter was the soda fountain counter. In its Golden Age (circa 1880–1914), the soda fountain's popularity made it an added value for every business that catered to the public's appetite. Every hotel, tearoom, department store, and candy shop joined the fountain party. (We've even seen photos of dates on skates canoodling at a rink-side fountain.)

But there's a reason why we think of the drugstore when we think of Mom and Pop and the first float they shared with two straws: floats came from soda fountains, and soda fountains came from drugstores. The fountain culture is an outgrowth of public medicine. The soda fountain is a child of Rx.

A brief history of medicinal drugs in America starts with Cherokee medicine men and conquistador alchemists, both of whom tried and failed to find a root, herb, or seed pod that would protect the natives from smallpox and the European explorers from the fevers of the New World. In the early days of settlement, a shortage of pharmacists prompted colonial authorities to offer free trans-Atlantic transport for would-be apothecaries, but there were few takers. Disease was rampant. Cures were primitive.

However, there was one pre-Industrial Era medical practice that stood the test of time—one that the first colonists shared with the Native Americans who hospitably introduced their visitors to sacred springs. Belief in the healing powers of the earth's natural mineral waters sent explorers and settlers to mountain springs as early as the 1600s.

By the end of the Civil War, a cadre of American physicians schooled in both chemistry and medicine was better empowered to address the ailments of the modern age. Of particular interest was the effectiveness of morphine and other narcotics in soothing soldiers and war widows alike (and which, for a few decades of unregulated libation, found a happy home in the soda fountain). But no amount of scientific discovery could shake that favorite and

ancient prescription: whether the complaint was nausea, nerves, lumbago, or lethargy, the well-to-do American was advised to "take the cure" at a nearby hot spring. In fact, hydrotherapy went beyond bathing; interest in mineral water included imbibing.

"Carbonated water stimulates circulation and respiration," wrote Jacob Baur in 1909. Baur, an entrepreneur from Terre Haute, Indiana, became a leading evangelist of the soda water trade. "Carbon is one of the principal strength-giving elements of food, and carbonic gas in soda water is undoubtedly a food as well as a tonic and stomachic."

But to fully realize the public health potential of this wonder-water, someone had to first figure out how to make it flow from a tap as easily as from a volcanic spring. This was a goal that amateur chemists had pursued for centuries by tinkering with ways to reproduce naturally effervescent water in the laboratory.

The Dutch botanist Herman Boerhaave was extracting carbon dioxide from chalk in the early 1700s. By the end of that century, sparkling water was a favorite scientific endeavor across Europe. In Britain, a clergyman named Joseph Priestly was "impregnating" water with gas—a feat denounced by righteous neighbors as "alchemy," (he fled with his bubbles to Pennsylvania in 1792). The French-man Antoine Lavoisier divined the chemical com-position of carbon dioxide before losing his head to the guillotine during the French Revolution. In 1770, the chemist Tobern Bergman presented the Royal Academy of Science with something not unlike Alka-Seltzer and dispatched it to remote Arctic communities to test its healthful properties. Ten years later, Jacob Schweppe, a German jeweler, invented a prototype carbonator to infuse drinking water with "fixed air."

In 1806, Benjamin Silliman, an American chemistry professor and reputed hypochondriac, took the cure at Saratoga Springs, New York. He

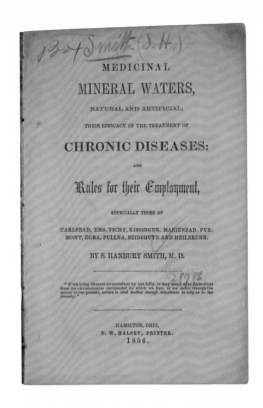

came away determined to make mineral water available to the masses who could not afford a trip to the spa. As a seminal figure in American academia and eventual founder of the *American Journal of Science*, Silliman deserves the benefit of the doubt about his altruistic motives (even if, at the time, he was a struggling professor with a clear interest in the health of his income). Suffice it to say that Silliman was among the first men to take up what was destined to be America's role in the history of man-made soda water: commercialization.

Silliman started a modest business selling carbonated water through a local apothecary in New Haven, Connecticut. Stymied by an inability to find bottles that didn't explode under pressure, he set his sights on public taprooms as distributors of his manufactured seltzers. In 1809, he opened the first public soda fountain at the Tontine Coffeehouse on Wall Street in New York City. With the installation of Silliman's improved apparatus for "aerating" water, carbonated water

was served alongside the stronger drinks already in demand by the stockbrokers and businessmen of the district. It was a commercial flop—even when Silliman deigned to allow his healthful sparkling waters to be used as mixers for the wines on the Tontine's menu.

In part, Silliman's failure was the result of stiff competition. His chief rival in New York, an Irishman named George Usher, one-upped him by staying open on Sundays, catering to ladies, and investing in superior equipment that kept his seltzers cold and uniformly bubbly. A later competitor, John Matthews, dealt Silliman a further blow when he got a jump on the purchase of every bit of scrap marble made available during the construction of St. Patrick's Cathedral. Marble dust, when mixed with sulphuric acid and purified, was an excellent source of carbonic gas and agitated well with water. Matthews reportedly manufactured twenty-five

million gallons of soda water from the scrap heap of that cathedral; Silliman got bupkis.

Meanwhile, in Philadelphia, soda peddlers were joining the ranks fast and furiously. Joseph Hawkins and Abraham Cohen were doing a swift business selling seltzers by "subscription:" $1.50 a month entitled the buyer to one glass per day. A French perfumer, Eduard Roussel, set up shop on the same street as Hawkins and Cohen. His innovation—lemon-flavored syrup—quickly found dozens of copycats. Two other Philadelphians, Townsend Speakman and Philip Physick, were adding fruit flavors to their product and selling them as the "Neophyte Julep."

In America's cities, soda carts were becoming common, pushing soda out onto the streets; in the smaller towns and the countryside, traveling salesmen peddled mineral waters along with their patent medicines and snake oils. But the truth is, none of these early entrepreneurs fared much better than Silliman. The early years of the soda fountain as a business venture were marked by trial and error, including formulas using sulphuric acid and calcium carbonate that were so off as to be explosive; batches of flat water that turned blood red from overoxidation in lead-lined tanks; water that turned toxic from being leached with lime and other less-than-salubrious solutions. There were races to the patent house, lawsuits, bankruptcy, and more than one suicide.

"In the soda fountain industry, competition has always been keen," wrote William S. Adkins, a prolific contributor to pharmacy journals. Writing in 1911, just a hundred years after the birth of the business, he noted only "two or three of the pioneer names still remain before the public; most of them, however, are gone."

Not so much gone, as swept aside by the swell of their progeny. Because even as soda water and its primitive and problematic dispensers were driving young businessmen to ruin, the market was gaining a thirst. According to one English journalist who visited Philadelphia in 1819, "The first thing every American who can afford five cents takes, on rising in the morning, is a glass of soda water."

By the time Adkins could remark on the forgotten pioneers, there were an estimated 125,000 soda fountains operating across the country. The American clientele, wrote one observer approvingly, feels "no harm to 'have a soda' about as often as one pleases, even if that means 'steen dozen times a day." If the pioneers of this daily digestive failed to make it a lucrative business, they had certainly succeeded in making it a popular one.

———

American pharmacists were the agents of soda's turn-of-the century popularity. Just like the physician with his penchant for prescribing "the baths," the pharmacist found a useful remedy in mineral

waters. Medicines at that time were administered in liquid form. Cures for headache, constipation, anxiety, or "female trouble" were dispensed discretely (particularly once soda water became a popular mask and mixer). One could step out to the corner drugstore (or send a boy if indisposed), and with a brief description of the symptoms, a neatly wrapped package of liquid medicine was passed across the counter. Relief came with a receipt.

Some of these remedies were harmless concoctions or virtual placebos. Others had real palliative qualities. Many of them were derived from substances that would be soon be outlawed by the 1906 Pure Food and Drugs Act—a federal law that was the first step in regulating intoxicants and narcotics. In the twilight of the nineteenth century, straight-laced citizens found an outlet in the opiates and barbiturates sanctioned by the pharmacist and delivered over the counter—an astounding array of tonics and serums made from heroin, morphine, cocaine, and even strychnine. The pharmacist was more than a lifesaver; he was mother's little helper

and father's secret weapon. Give him a siphon of soda water to mix up those opiates and a seat at the counter and indeed, he soon had patrons who "felt no harm" in having a soda. Or two or three. In industry parlance, the "soda fiend" was his most loyal customer.

It was the druggist who most keenly recognized the fountain's potential and did his utmost to ensure its popularity. "An elegant pharmacy," forecast one expert in a 1908 issue of *The Phamaceutical Era*, "will mean the preparation of nauseous drugs in such palatable form that they will all be dispensed at the soda fountain." Baur, the gastricly challenged inventor of liquid carbonic gas, was a second-generation pharmacist. His innovation allowed drugstore owners to carbonate their own soda water in-house at a tenth of the cost. The soda fountain became profitable. And pharmacists became mixologists.

These were the prerequisites for the soda fountain boom. Once "soda" came not just with castor oil, but with syrup, sugar, and coca wine, and was served up in a tall glass with a dollop of ice cream or spoonful of pineapple—well, nobody was sending a boy to fetch their medicine any more. They were making personal appearances at the pharmacy, clamoring for a seat at the counter.

"Want to increase your sales by 50 percent?" asked De Forest Saxe in 1898. Saxe's best-selling guide, *Hints to Soda Water Dispensers,* guaranteed "both money and reputation" to druggists who "properly served and pushed" his proprietary formulae. Among them was Saxe's Phospho-Guarana, touted as "the greatest thirst-quencher in the world," thanks, no doubt to the celery, but also to the Amazonian stimulant, guarana.

"Nervous people will come like clockwork three (3) times a day for their drink when they once learn its value," he promised. Not quite "'steen dozen," but a healthy business, nonetheless.

———

By no means was the sale of barbiturate "nervines" and stimulating coca recipes the sole cause of the soda fountain's extraordinary boom. On the contrary, creative competition and a drive to serve the diverse tastes of the American public helped create one of the largest menus in our national history.

A seemingly endless variety of libations and concoctions flowed from the soda fountain during its century of prominence. From the introduction of "hot sodas," which allowed soda fountains to turn a profit in the off season, when cocoa was more attractive than ice cream, to the happy accident that

LEGENDS OF THE SODA FOUNTAIN:
DE FOREST SAXE

De Forest Saxe was soda's first evangelist. Like most players in this story, he was a pharmacist by trade. Saxe believed that the soda fountain was America's El Dorado, and he was ready to share the wealth. In an era when most druggists jealously guarded their proprietary formulae and "secret recipes," Saxe bucked the trend. His 1898 *Hints to Soda Water Dispensers* was the first comprehensive recipe book for soda fountain owners.

"Drinks, which if properly served and pushed will make you both money and reputation," was the subhead of his three-dollar tract—the fruit of seventeen years experimentation in carbonation. The guide, a comprehensive menu of still drinks, phosphates, nervines, and "vitalizers," promised to not just increase sales but ensure that loyal customers show up "like clockwork" to sate their thirst.

Saxe began his adventures in soda dispensing in 1879, when he bought a failing drug store in Omaha, Nebraska, along with all its stock. He struggled to make the business profitable, and then took a long hard look at a competitor on the block who had a fountain of his own: "I came to the conclusion that if [he] could capture all, or almost all, of the soda trade by simply making better drinks than anyone else in the business, I would see what I could do . . ."

In the first year, claimed Saxe, the soda business doubled his profit. The next season he advertised and found sales "surpassing my most sanguine expectations." Next came the upgrades: a generator, a full-size canopy-top counter, and a selection of "hot sodas." By 1890, Saxe was making fifteen thousand dollars yearly on his Omaha soda business. He sold it and moved to Chicago, where he lobbied pharmacists to invest in state-of-the-art fountain technologies and modern soda recipes to stay profitable and popular.

Saxe wasn't the only soda man to shill his recipes. Once the ice cream soda was an undisputed cornerstone of American commerce, there were hundreds of booklets, brochures, and recipe pamphlets to encourage uniformity of preparation. Not to mention trade journals, which were pumping out new recipes monthly.

But Saxe was the pioneer.

More importantly, he's back. That's right, Saxe's *Hints* were re-released in 2010 by Nabu Press, just in time to lead a bona-fide revival in old-school fountain drinks.

Here are a few of his formulae :

NO. 42.

DIAMOND SYRUP.

Vanilla Syrup	-	1 pt.
Pineapple Syrup	-	1 "
Lemon Syrup	-	1 "
Honey, strained	-	2 oz.
Fruit Acid	-	⅛ "
Eggs, well beaten	-	3 in number
Gum Foam	-	3 teaspoonfuls.
Phospho Guarana Syrup		1 pt.
Mix.		

This makes an excellent combination and a good seller.

NO. 92.

BOSTON FLIP.

Use one ounce Don't Care Syrup, one whole egg, teaspoonful lemon juice, half teaspoonful acid phosphate, teaspoonful sugar (or more if necessary), a little cracked ice. Then fill glass with plain soda and proceed as in making almond sponge, only do not shake the drink.

gave us the sundae, innovation and steady demand for new tastes and recipes kept the soda fountain menu ever evolving. Some concoctions would prove to be perennial favorites; others had a shorter lifespan ("clam cordial," anyone?) In any case, by the turn of the twentieth century, a successful soda fountain could be expected to serve no less than forty different libations at any given time.

This was because the clientele of the fountain had come to include all circles of the American people—young and old, male and female, well-to-do and just getting by. The menu needed something for everyone. (Or better yet, more than a dozen somethings for everyone.)

Huge demand meant sizable profits for the pharmacy. While an average fountain drink might cost a nickel or a dime in 1910, the total sales of carbonated drinks that year surpassed the federal budget for the army and navy. Americans spent

$500 million at the soda fountain that year. The soda fountain, which had started as a sideline business, now dominated the pharmacist's trade. Even in small-town America, a proprietor could report "our fountain made more than our entire store last year."

Detractors lamented this turn of events, worrying that the soda fountain had seduced the pharmacist from his respected role. "Pharmacies are fast losing their identity as drug stores," rued William Miller Bartlett, a self-proclaimed "Ethical Drug Store Owner" from Salem, Massachusetts. "The compounding of medicine and sale thereof is, apparently, an insignificant and unimportant part of the general business conducted therein," sniffed Bartlett, concluding that the mortar and pestle had given way to the soda sign.

Physically, too, the soda fountain had left its utilitarian roots behind. From a simple goose-necked

tap pumping healthful carbonated gas from a barrel in the cellar, the turn-of-the-century soda fountain had become a resplendent (and often gaudy) machine, gussied up in all the finery of the age.

"Glitz sold soda water," concludes historian Ann Funderburg in her history, *Sundae Best*. The fountains of the day, in keeping with the era's artistic admirations, featured onyx, mirrors, and either a frieze of water nymphs or a rotating cupid. With names like The France, The Albion, or The Adriatic, these fountains were sold both as cutting edge technology and objets d'art.

Drugstore owners were captivated. Most subscribed to the notion that bigger (and brassier) was better and invested heavily in the latest designs. That meant that furnishings had to keep up, and soon the establishment was sporting mahogany tables and player pianos. The soda fountain had both surpassed and seduced the drugstore to become a

symbol of the Gilded Era itself, the last two decades of the nineteenth century.

Not everyone who came to the counter sought a cure or a simple thirst-quencher. Many came for company and culture. That, after all, is the soda fountain's legacy and what we celebrate at Brooklyn Farmacy. Long after "soda water" was removed from the U.S. Pharmacopoeia as a pharmaceutical product, we still view our fountain as a dispenser of remedies. We may not whip up lactics and pepsins, but we do believe that an ice cream soda in the company of friends is the eternal over-the-counter medicine.

THE SODA FOUNTAIN COMES FROM Rx

CHAPTER TWO

A GOLDEN AGE

The life of the American soda fountain was a briefer wonder than we realize—less than a century from start to finish, from about 1860 until World War II. Throughout its short history, the fountain was ever changing—a sweet and sticky work in progress. But there was a moment, we think, when the fountain had it absolutely right. An instant when the sundae was festooned and about to be consumed—that cherry-on-the-top moment. So let's indulge a little and linger over the Golden Age of the soda fountain.

To get to the cherry, first you have to calibrate the carbonate. Then you need to chill the taps, add some flavored syrups, and tuck those opiates back behind the locked vitrines. You must wait for every man, child, grandmother, and out-of-towner to know that a five-cent thirst quencher is to be had around the corner. You have to persuade your customers to nod in agreement when told that adding a raw egg or a dollop of fresh cream makes a drink "fancy." Next you wait for ice cream to become just as handy as soda and for any number of contenders to claim to have invented the "sundae" (there's a rather long list of them).

Then you can take a short rest and let the entrepreneurs do their thing—you know, all those gunners who see millions to be made in a better straw dispenser, a sanitary glass tumbler, or a countertop ice shaver. Next up, a little social consciousness: let's get the anti-alcohol brigade on board to promote soda as the "temperance champagne—invigorating but not intoxicating." Now, just hold on two more secs—long enough for American men to appreciate the fountain's quick service and for the fairer sex to cotton to its convenience as an acceptable place to socialize without a chaperone.

What's that you say? There's a line out the door? It's 1875 and the ice cream soda is a smash hit. There's a fountain in just about every city in America, dispensing an average of twelve hundred glasses a day.

Is this the cherry-on-top moment?

Almost. Yes. We're just about there.

———

The true Golden Age of the American soda fountain corresponds with the so-called Gilded Age—the last twenty years of the nineteenth century when Americans embraced money, industry, and fashion like never before (but we won't say "since").

The late 1870s and 1880s were years when America, done licking her Civil War wounds, started training to be a global superpower. The economy boomed and industry quintupled, extracting resources, filling factories, and building railroads to do so. For enterprising and ambitious investors, it was a time of massive returns. Ruthless "Captains of Industry"—Rockefellers, Carnegies, and Vanderbilts—became almost unthinkably wealthy, monopolizing the businesses of steel, oil, and steam engines, while social progressives built up their own head of steam over the widening inequity between these "robber barons" and the waves of destitute immigrants who came to mine their ore and shine their shoes.

The fashions of the time reflected the quality of the wealth being created: new, flashy, excessive. It could be seen in the glittering mansions of Newport, Rhode Island, where modern millionaires built their cliffside colony of nouveau chateaux; it could be seen in the lavish New York City parties of the Astors and Fishes; but it could also be seen, on a more populist but equally puffed-up display, in the polished marble and sparkling brass of the soda fountain.

"Style, I find, has many devout worshippers," soda hawker George Usher advised his rather styleless partner, Benjamin Silliman, in the early days of the business. By the 1870s, ambitious fountain owners had taken this maxim to heart, discarding their simple goose-necked taps and cellar carbonators for custom-made furnishings that hid the mechanics of the pumps behind gas lamps, chandeliers, statuary, and stained glass. Once a humble countertop dispenser of carbonated water, the soda fountain was

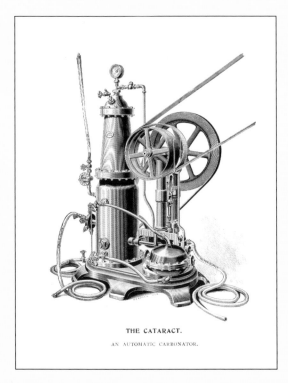

THE CATARACT.

AN AUTOMATIC CARBONATOR.

AGORA

Confectionery Menu

Agora's Deluxe ICE CREAM & SHERBET

Ice Cream Flavors

Vanilla	Chocolate Chip	Chocolate Almond
Chocolate	Vanilla Fudge	Pineapple Coconut
Coffee	Banana	Rum Raisin
Strawberry	Cherry Vanilla	Peach
Butter Pecan	Pistachio	Irish Coffee
Chocolate Mint Chip	Peppermint Stick	Maple Walnut
	German Chocolate Fudge Cake	

Sherbet Flavors

Orange	Lemon	Raspberry

ICE CREAM OR SHERBET .60
Double portion 1.10

Ice Cream Sodas

Birch Beer	Creme de Menthe	Choc. Mint
Vanilla	Orange	Cinnamon
Chocolate	Sarsaparilla	Wintergreen
Root Beer	Cherry	Peppermint
Lemon	Coffee	Maple Walnut
Lime		Broadway

1.00

SODAS – SPECIAL FLAVORS

Strawberry, Blueberry, Raspberry, Pineapple,
Coffee Royale, Coffee Rum, Maple Walnut,
Cherry Rum, Daiquiri, Angostura Pineapple   1.25

Super Size ice cream sodas

2.25

Banana Splits

2.00   3.00   4.00

LEGENDS OF THE SODA FOUNTAIN:
JAMES WALKER TUFTS

Like many of the men who made their fortunes in the Gilded Age, James Walker Tufts was a man in a hurry. He got on the soda bandwagon early, sending in his order for one of the very first models of the Dows Ice Cream Soda Apparatus , which had a built in ice shaver in addition to a seltzer spigot and syrup taps. He would have to wait, he was told. There was a long list of buyers ahead of him.

So Tufts, trained both as an apothecary and a silversmith, built his own. By the time he was thirty, his Boston-based Arctic Soda Fountain Company was a leading purveyor of high-end fountains and fountain supplies, with display rooms in Chicago and New York.

It was Tufts who foisted kitsch on the fountain when he gave the countertop apparatus a mansard roof and a chimney that sprouted a bouquet of flowers. He soon designed a whole line of so-called "cottage" fountains in an assortment of faux architectural styles.

Tufts' design went from miniature to magnificent with his monumental Arctic Pavilion, the most bombastic of a dozen lavish fountains he commissioned for the 1876 Philadelphia Centennial Exhibition. Certain that the Centennial was the key to his fortune, Tufts paid fifty thousand dollars for exclusive rights to sell soda waters on site. His cornering of the Centennial soda market, if not as cutthroat as a Vanderbilt or a Rockefeller, was a bold move nonetheless: a more than a million dollar outlay for a ten-cent drink.

At the end of the Centennial, Tufts reported a loss on the fair, but flourishing business nationwide more than made up for it. When the leading fountain manufacturers joined forces in 1891 to create the American Soda Fountain Company, they made Tufts its first president.

Four years later, troubled by asthma and ill health, Tufts left the business in his son's hands and headed south into a busy retirement. He bought six hundred acres of North Carolina land and embarked on a new venture, hiring the firm of Central Park's landscaper, Frederick Olmstead, and a team of master builders to transform the scrubland into a "natural paradise" and a premiere health resort. In the plans, he included a nine-hole golf course—despite his peers' dismissal of the game as a "passing fancy."

James Tufts died in 1902 at his beloved Pinehurst, home of world-champion golf. In his will, he remembered the foremen of his soda fountain factory, leaving them five hundred dollars each. To the rest of us he left two great (and leisurely) American pastimes.

Want Ads

now a resplendent display across the length of the counter. Installed directly into a wall, and paneled with mahogany, marble, and mirrors, the fountain had become an altar for the Victorian fashionista.

Which brings us to the cherry—the Arctic Pavilion.

Billed as "the largest and most magnificent soda water apparatus in the world," the Tufts Arctic Pavilion was a three-story, thirty-ton behemoth, serving tens of thousands of daily patrons during the 1876 Philadelphia Centennial. The massive installation boasted a tropical forest colonnaded by 104 spigots and "an immense ice-cavern reached by a flight of stairs." This king daddy fountain was more than just an oversize opportunity to slake your thirst; the Arctic Pavilion was a veritable beverage ecosphere, a soda spectacle, a monument to a business as booming as the times.

Granted, we never stood in line to sample the Arctic Pavilion's wares. Sadly, the only extant image of the thing is pen and ink artists' renderings. And yet the lack of photographic evidence only enhances the mythical standing of the great Arctic Pavilion, which is our idea of the cherry-on-top moment. Or maybe cherry-over-the-top moment. Definitely an "it doesn't get better than this" moment.

———

The Philadelphia Centennial, the second World's Fair to be held on American soil, was launched on opening day by President Ulysses S. Grant. It was a good bit of symbolism—the conquering general inviting all of Europe to admire the innovations and inventions that had vaulted the United States ahead of France and Great Britain just a scant decade after his army had restored the Union from Civil War.

On display across the 285 acres of Philadelphia's Fairmount Park as evidence of American global greatness were a cable from the Brooklyn Bridge, the Corliss steam engine, early prototypes of the telephone and the typewriter, and the disembodied right arm of the as-yet-to-be-assembled Statue of Liberty.

At the time of the Centennial, one hundred thousand soda fountains were serving up eight million drinks a year, and those numbers were rising fast. The fountain's popularity can't be attributed solely to the American public's thirst for sweet, fizzy water. Much of the credit goes to a slightly more complex appetite: the desire to spend money. The promise of the growing consumer class was much ballyhooed in Philadelphia that summer; luxury goods and practical wares were as proudly displayed as the miraculous electric light bulb. Not for nothing was the main exhibition designed to invoke that exciting new public gathering space, the department store.

Counting on buyers, a whole new breed of sellers emerged—and many of them eyeballed

the soda fountain. If one trade magazine declared that "the thinking public believes in the drink!," another was quick to add that "thousands of wide-awake people are getting rich" by serving up sodas. As the fountain matured from a fad to a phenom to a national institution, a steady stream of druggists clamored to set up their counters and keep them up to date. Syrup purveyors knocked down their doors with samples and the assurance "it's a good thing, push it along." And fountain manufacturers scrambled to outfit the mushrooming soda shops. As the Low Art Tile Company reported in the *The Pharmaceutical Era*, entering the soda fountain trade compelled a business to "run their works to the full capacity night and day to fill their orders."

By 1876, four manufacturers dominated the supply of wall fountains and fountain appliances: New York's John Matthews Jr.; Philadelphia's own

John Lippincott; and from Boston, A. J. Puffer and James W. Tufts. To protect their profits in a booming business, the four joined together to form the American Soda Fountain Company. By 1892, the combined sales of the American Soda Fountain Company topped three million dollars.

Meanwhile, Jacob Baur of the Liquid Carbonic Company was blazing his own path to the top as the leading nation's leading supplier of CO_2 cylinders with his own line of fountains and syrup as well. Bauer died at the peak of his success, just twenty years after his initial seventy-five-thousand-dollar investment to found Liquid Carbonic. His wife was a four-million-dollar widow.

At the same time in Chicago, a former drugstore clerk named Charles Walgreen was opening his first pharmacy, the first in an enterprise that would quickly become the nation's fastest growing franchise business, thanks in large part to its soda fountain. Walgreen asserted that his drugstore's fountain was "the magnet that operated every hour . . . ." Walgreen was on to something; his faith in the fountain was the basis for a pharmacy empire that thrived even through the Great Depression to become the country's preeminent drugstore chain and one of the Fortune 500 largest American companies.

The Gilded Age captains of industry that you learned about in the history books controlled steel, oil, and natural gas. But to that, you may add carbonic gas.

———

Of course you don't get to be a millionaire just by making egg creams down on the corner. (Believe us, we're trying.) But during the fountain's heyday, it wasn't too hard to "make soda water pay the rent," according to the manager of a high-end fountain in Buffalo, New York. There was only one Walgreen in this business, but the fountain had tapped a seemingly unquenchable thirst in America and as such was considered a "consistent money-maker" for anyone in the business for decades to come.

"It is not a business that needs any intricate organization, but rather common sense and constructive management," coached *The Soda Fountain* monthly in 1926, a year when total receipts from fountains across the nation closed in on a half-billion dollars. For drugstore owners with those skills, the addition of a fountain was a no-brainer to boost the bottom line. For proprietors lacking managerial skills and common sense, there was a whole library of trade journals to help. There was also a burgeoning soda-consultancy business. Because it might not occur to you that if you rely on direct mail marketing you will fail to reach the most important customer—the woman of the house, whose name did not appear in turn-of-the-century address directories. Nor might it be common sense that papers and magazines are no-no's at the fountain, as they "remind one too much of a saloon." Who knew?

WHO YOU CALLING A JERK?

First Known Use of SODA JERK / 1922
From *Merriam-Webster*
soda jerk (*noun*):
a person who dispenses carbonated drinks and ice cream at a soda fountain.
Also called a "soda jerker"

It's one of our favorite aspects of the soda fountain. That we get to call ourselves "jerks" with pride and impunity.

Originally, the guy who ran the soda fountain was known as a "dispenser," for he was as crucial as a mechanical piece of the fountain itself. As the term "jerk" entered the popular lexicon in the 1920s, some fountain owners frowned on a name they believed lacked dignity.

Miss Wahle, manager of several Kroger Grocery Fountains in Cincinnati, told her employees: "I will fire [you] quicker for using the term 'soda jerker' or 'soda squirt' than for anything else."

At Brooklyn Farmacy, we think a "jerk" is an honorary title—to be bestowed on fountain employees (and customers) of the highest order. In fact, if you come into our store wearing one of our Jerk T-shirts, you get a free egg cream. How is that for a jerk move?

Naturally, good service was as crucial as common sense for true success. Whether as a side business or a stand-alone operation, the soda fountain was no longer the purview of the pharmacist. It had to be staffed by a competent dispenser, the immortal soda "jerk." There was a lot riding on this new breed of barman. Traffic in the leading fountains of New York, Chicago, and Boston required a soda dispenser to pull up to ten glasses a minute at peak hours. A small town druggist risked losing fastidious regulars if his counterman didn't keep the bar as sparkling as the patrons' own kitchen sinks, and you might as well just shut your doors if your fountain man couldn't accommodate a patron's personal notion of the perfect soda—you know, the one that he had last week while visiting relatives in Birmingham? What was it called, Mabel? A tangerette fruit shrub?

That brings us to perhaps the single most important asset of a good soda fountain jerk (after clean nails and a friendly smile): creativity.

Ever since an added raw egg or a dollop of cream turned plain soda into a "Fancy Drink," the fountain menu was in constant evolution. The offerings of a turn-of-the-century fountain were myriad, marvelous, and often, to the twenty-first century ear, mysterious. "A few years ago the call was for plain soda, with some kind of flavored syrup. Now there is no limit to the kinds of drinks—in some stores from fifty to seventy-five," wrote the *American Druggist and Pharmaceutical Record* in 1906. "The stores that vary and offer new drinks secure the best business. It is said that some of the most successful drinks are concocted on the spur of the moment."

For example, the ice cream soda was born when a harried vendor ran out of fresh cream, and the ice cream cone was a joint venture of an ice cream vendor and a waffle seller who were neighbors at the 1904 St. Louis World's Fair. Meanwhile the sundae—an ice cream soda without the soda— was undergoing daily metamorphoses and had a permanent place on the menu under various guises and names. Perennial favorites—root beer, ginger ale, cream soda, and the like—shared top billing with "spoon novelties" and concoctions named for whatever fad was sweeping the nation, be it the bicycle, the Brooklyn Bridge, the pineapple, or the exploration of the South Pole.

Gone were the days when dispensers jealously guarded their "proprietary formulae." Now, they sold them. A typical collection of printed and bound recipes sold for $1.25 and was hawked with a cautionary tale: "Don't fill your customers up with gelatin and soap bark. Make sure your clerk has the most up to date Guide for Soda Dispensers. He'll be worth twice as much to you." Another dispenser offered "A Fancy Drink from Every State," including the Colorado Sangaru, the Michigan Lemonade (with ginger, spearmint, and raspberry vinegar), New Jersey Fluff (fruit juice and whipping cream), the Indian Territory soufflé, and in a prescient moment, Alaska Gold.

A good soda dispenser was expected to know the standards by heart, be abreast of the trending favorites, whip up a custom drink to perfection, and experiment with fruitful results. Like a master bartender, the classic dispenser was a beverage artiste or, as a 1945 article preferred, "a fountain chemist."

"Our Soda Jerks are Licensed Fizzicians," punned a fountain in Winslow, Arizona, displaying the lighthearted touch that was also expected of a first-rate soda man. Fizzicians, after all, should be bit of a showman—tossing glasses and breaking eggs one-handed.

Oh, and one more thing: He had to be nice to the customers. *All* the customers.

———

The drugstore counter was one of the first places in America where it was acceptable and expected for men and women, children and adults to congregate. It was a truly democratic establishment,

a "community social center" in the words of fountain historian Anne Funderburg.

Yes, there are disclaimers to be made: America at the turn of the century was not class-less. Nor was it free of racist and sexist biases. Xenophobia was rampant in New York and other cities absorbing a fresh wave of immigrants. Racism was ubiquitous and codified into law in the Jim Crow South where African-Americans were excluded from being patrons in soda fountains, even as they were welcomed as dishwashers. These are the warts of American history, and they are visible even in her most inclusive and inviting social spaces.

That said, the fountain was a particular venue for social progress and democratic reform, linked closely with gains made for women during the Suffrage Movement and for African-Americans who made the fountain's successor, the lunch counter, their pulpit of protest. Many of the immigrants who moved westward in search of the American dream knit their entrepreneurial strength into the social fabric of the ethnic communities they founded: German bakeries in Cincinnati, Greek grocers in Minneapolis, and Lithuanian diners outside of Chicago all incorporated the soda fountain into their street-front establishments. If there was one place where the patronage of every demographic was courted, it was the soda fountain—the most inclusive and socially accepted social gathering place.

In its Golden Age, the soda fountain was where a society dame, a governess, a working girl, and an actress would sit at a single counter alongside a banker, a newsboy, and a taxi hack. For Victorian women who wanted to "get out of the house" but also wanted to feel at home, the fountain embraced the furnishings, values, and civility of the time. For Midwestern families with modest cultural strivings, that same environment offered "the first realization of the beauties of art and glories of architecture." Men loved the quick pick-me-up. Kids loved the even quicker soda, gone in a flash. And whether you were a magnate or a milliner, you might be enticed to try the latest flavors.

This is why the soda jerk had to serve all comers with a smile. Because as *Soda Fountain* magazine reminded its readers, even "the grubby urchin who is now sticky with lolly-pop . . . in a few short years will be transformed into an immaculate youth with irreproachable trouser creases, wise in high school lore, and with a tendency to bring his best girl to consume marshmallow sundaes at the fountain."

If that's not the Great American dream, what is?

CLAM SODA AND OTHER IMPROBABLE PRODUCTS OF THE FOUNTAIN

The creativity of the soda fountain knew no bounds. And sometimes, it would seem, had no taste. Here are some recipes that did not stand the test of time:

- Celery Egg Tonic
- Mincemeat Ice Cream
- Pru-Nut Malted Milk (that's prunes and walnuts)
- Mousse de Sux Sundae ("a dandy seller at 25 cents")
- Chartreuse: Oil of Melissa, Saffron, Oil of Calamus, all filtered through talcum
- Yeast Milkshake
- Caramel Cream Sundae on a bed of lettuce

Among the weirdest fountain menu items we have found are those of the once-hot "Hot Soda" variety:

- Pulp de Marron (chestnuts)
- Hot Egg Phosphate
- Egg & Coffee

Not to mention these doozies from the earliest soda fountain lunch menus:

- American Cheese and Peanut Butter
- Hamburger, Egg, and Orange Marmalade on Nut Bread
- Peanut butter, Sardine, and Potato Salad on Rye
- Cider Gelatin Salad
- Pineapple Crabmeat Cocktail

Other Spoon Novelties we think we shan't see again are those that you really "had to be there" for:

- "Sprocket Foam," "Cycla-Phate," and "Pedal Pusher" owed their popularity to the biggest thing in Gilded Era leisure—the bicycle.
- The "Yes We Have No Bananas" Sundae was named for a smash-hit song. Even modern customers who recognize the reference might be confused by this recipe, which calls for both bananas and banana syrup. But maybe that's the point?
- Ping Pong Sundae
- College Soda (because it will never mean anything other than "cheap beer" again)
- Lindbergh Glide (for Lucky Lindy, the famed aviator)

Of course, we can't honestly assert that the post-fountain sodas have been catastrophe free. Here are some god-awful sodas of today that were shelved pretty quickly after they hit the stores:

- Pepsi Ice Cucumber (a seller only in Japan)
- Pepsi Blue (customer review: "file it in same category as Plax and Listerine")
- Jones Brussels Sprout (part of a holiday pack that included Turkey and Gravy and Wild Herb Stuffing)
- Diet Cherry Vanilla Dr. Pepper (review: "why not add 3 more flavors to DP's boasted 23?")
- Bacon Soda (from the makers of Buffalo Wings and Sweet Corn sodas)

CHAPTER THREE

PROHIBITION AND THE JAZZ AGE FOUNTAIN

Prohibition, the culmination of a century of antialcohol activism, went into effect on January 1, 1920. When it did, every bar, tavern, and saloon in the country was out of business. The already packed soda fountain was about to get even more crowded as patrons made room for bereft barflies. Thirteen years later, the nation ushered beer and then booze back into legality with little of the fanfare that accompanied its banishment. This languid reunion was evidence that America had never really quit alcohol, no matter what the Eighteenth Amendment said. But it also spoke to the soda fountain's ability to absorb much of the saloon's purpose. Because when the owners of post-Prohibition fountains had to decide whether

PLEASE PROTECT US

By Voting Against Liquor

100,000 boys are needed every year to recruit the army of drunkards.

You can no more run a saloon without destroying boys than you can run a saw mill without logs.

The saloon takes the boy that has been nursed and cared for by a loving mother, the boy with bright hopes and prospects, and for the sake of profits and taxes, turns him into a drunkard, a vagabond and an outcast.

When you vote for liquor you vote against our homes, against our women and children, your vote licenses a death-trap for every boy in the State.

Protect the boys by voting against liquor on the 26th of May.

to add a beer tap to their soda pumps, most opted not to. They had built up a flourishing trade on wholesome, economical, sanitary service that was, to the industry's mind, "beer-proof."

Wherever you stood on the relative merits of seltzer over spirits, Prohibition—the thirteen-year-long American experiment in abstention—gave new context to the soda fountain as the nation's watering hole.

It wasn't hard to see it coming. Alcohol was a frontline battle in the nineteenth century "culture wars," and a lopsided fight at that. On one side was a disciplined army of true believers with fire in their bellies and money in their coffers. On the other side was an amorphous body of complacent libertarians—tipplers who took their right to raise a glass for granted and brewers who underestimated the determination of the Prohibitionists.

That determination came from decades of failed attempts to get the country's drinkers to self-moderate. Beginning with the first *Sermon to Gentlemen Upon Temperance and Exercise*, published in 1772, the temperance movement ebbed and flowed right up to the ratification of the Eighteenth Amendment banning the sale, transport, and manufacture of alcohol. At times, it seemed a quixotic quest. The above-mentioned sermon, for example, was penned by Declaration of Independence signer Benjamin Rush, and marked the start of a lifelong campaign to save drinkers from, among other perditions, jaundice, horse racing, dropsy, prison, murder, madness, despair, and the gallows.

The question was, how to define "moderate"? Experts estimate that nineteenth-century Americans drank three times as much liquor as we do today. No less a national spokesperson than President Abraham Lincoln noted "intoxicating liquor [is] used by everybody, repudiated by nobody." According to modern-day social historian Eric Burns, "No other activity of the time, perhaps not even the conceiving and implementing of freedom itself, was as important . . . as the consumption of alcoholic beverages." By his reckoning, Americans drank night and day, spending a quarter of their household income on the stuff. A quick run through those moments in the Republic's founding that took place in a drinking-house, Burns concludes, is evidence that the tavern was "the most venerated of American institutions."

Maybe. But veneration gave way to repudiation as drinking habits turned from hard cider and small beer (ale that contained very little alcohol) to the stronger stuff like whiskey and rum. As the number of bars and saloons swelled, so did public disapproval. Once the tavern was seen taking a toll on household incomes, agricultural productivity, and marital harmony, "veneration" was termed "addiction," "inebriation" and "the damnation of drink." Fire-breathing temperance workers, many of whom were reformed alcoholics themselves, urged "denizens of the pit" to "snap [their] burning chains" and join in testimony against the evils of alcohol. The temperance movement was drawing new zealots—and to them, moderation was no longer sufficient.

With complete prohibition of the sale of alcohol as the goal, temperance activists worked with the "tenacity of bulldogs and patience of army ants," to move one state after the other into the dry column. In some places, the fight was won with literal battle-axes, like Carrie Nation's own, which she wielded with fanatical zeal against the saloons of Kansas. Elsewhere, a cool-headed approach prevailed: In Maine, the temperance drive was spearheaded by a Quaker, Neil Dows, whose efforts bore fruit in 1851 when Maine became the first state in the nation to prohibit the sale of alcohol. Vermont followed. By the time the U.S. Congress took it up and signed it into law, Prohibition was already a reality in more than half of the United States. And you can bet that the soda fountains in those states were doing brisk business.

It's no accident that the world's most successful soda was born in Atlanta, Georgia. That city, devastated at the end of the Civil War by General Sherman's army, rose quickly from the ashes. By 1885, Atlanta was the state's largest city and the only one to achieve Prohibition through popular referendum. That made Atlanta a thirsty market for a "soft drink" that could rival the kick of banned booze. Called the "city of fountains" (soda fountains, that is), Atlanta in the early 1900s had one on just about every corner. All of them were selling the wildly popular new soda invented by local pharmacist John Stith Pemberton.

Pemberton, a self-starter who cured his own addiction to morphine with the dubious help of cocaine, spent ten years in search of a patent medicine that would make him a wealthy man. He gave the world Pemberton's Extract of Stillingia and Globe Flower Cough Syrup before hitting on the formula that would be his legacy. It was a derivation of Vin Mariani, a popular "nervine" endorsed by "three Popes, Sarah Bernhardt, Thomas Edison, and William McKinley." Vin Mariani's fancy name belied a simple recipe: five parts Bordeaux, one part cocaine. The law-abiding Pemberton replaced the wine with extract of kola, an African nut with stimulating qualities and added soda water. Sarah Bernhardt and the pope never looked back. "Coca-Cola" was the new Vin Mariani.

Coca-Cola was only the most successful of thousands of branded "soft drinks" answering the call for "invigoration without intoxication." Also selling well were Moxie, Pepsin Punch, and Dr. Pepper, the last of which was tried by twenty

million people at the alcohol-free St. Louis World's Fair in 1904. Copycats seized on the exotic kola nut to produce their own variants. Some would attract a loyal local following. Few achieved national prominence: Christo Cola called itself "the nation's joy," but it was, at best, only Richmond, Virginia's joy; Texatone, a grapefruit-flavored soda from the creators of Dr. Pepper, never got too far out of Waco, Texas. In Missouri alone, one thousand different soft drinks were on the market. But the crowned king was Coca-Cola, which by 1920 sold seventeen million gallons per year in America—about six gallons for every man, woman, and child. Judging from the collection of photographs we've uncovered of early soda fountains, Pemberton's cola was flowing steadily through the American's soda fountains.

With the passage of the Eighteenth Amendment, even this was insufficient, according to *Soda Fountain* magazine. "There are not enough soft drinks being manufactured . . . to fill the void left by the decease of John Barleycorn," wrote the editors during the first year of Prohibition.

Soda would need to do better. And it would, with the help of ice cream, music, and the enduring American ability to maintain high spirits through low times.

––––––––

"Ice cream is a greater medium for the cause of temperance than all the sermons ever preached," crowed soda fountain proselytizers as America prepared to go dry. Billed as the "universal palliative to Prohibition," ice cream went from a popular item to an absolute necessity for twentieth-century soda shops. Menus gave the nickel ice cream cone top billing along with the nickel soda, and Americans bought two billion of the frozen treats in 1923. Sundae concoctions were limitless, and many found a place for those salty refugees from the tavern—peanuts and pretzels.

The rise of ice cream to the refreshment throne was most literally performed in the nation's breweries, many of which were rehabbed to live a second life as ice cream factories. This industrial conversion, combined with advances in refrigeration and mass production, helped triple ice cream manufacturing from 1914 to 1921. Trade magazines were insufficient resources for the booming business; avid ice cream enthusiasts could take college courses or become autodidacts with the help of textbooks like *The Ice Cream Laboratory Guide*.

The only downside to what looked like limitless ice cream profits came from the government, which needed to offset the cost of World War I and the loss of revenue from alcohol taxes. In 1919, an unprecedented luxury tax on sugar and soft drinks was introduced. At 10 percent, the tax was a new burden on soda fountain dispensers and bottled soft drink manufacturers alike, who vilified it as "manifestly unfair and inequitable."

Confectioners, bottlers, soda jerks, and ice cream parlors fought back against the notion that ice cream and other fountain treats should be considered luxuries. "Ice Cream Is a Healthy Food," declared one advertiser on the eve of the country's first National Ice Cream Day. "We have the assurance of physicians that sugar is a necessary food that's good for us," wrote another, brandishing various studies in the vitamin content of ice cream. So onerous was the levy that a former U.S. Senator, Thomas Hardwick, made a trip to Washington to lobby against a tax "upon the portion of the public least able to pay it." One assumes that the good senator, who by then was the acting governor of Georgia, was referring to the customers of the five-cent soda, and not to the owners of Georgia's golden goose—the Coca-Cola Company. At any rate, Hardwick failed and the tax prevailed, generating an annual fifteen million dollars from soda makers in federal revenue. Texas, home of Dr. Pepper and what appears to be the nation's sweetest tooth, paid the heaviest tab—in 1923 the state's record ice cream receipts totaled 10 percent of all ice cream sales in the country; one million glasses of Coca-Cola were sold that year at the Southland Pharmacy in Dallas alone.

Taxes be damned, Americans kept the soda fountain in clover through Prohibition and the rougher decade to follow. Having upped their daily dosage thirty times over since the turn of the century, they kept screaming for ice cream—as the insipid 1928 song assures us we all did. Well into the Great Depression, ice cream accounted for almost half of all the soda fountain's sales.

———

Thousands of barmen were out of work thanks to national Prohibition; the soda set were the beneficiaries, inheriting a brigade of competent and experienced employees. Speed, agility, and youth—the most sought-after traits of the old soda dispenser—were still valued, but the fountain had matured. It had to serve a bit of fun and camaraderie. Bartenders knew how to deliver. They knew how to talk to men (though it took some practice to get used to the women), and they knew how to convince them that whatever was ailing would pass. As one new customer saw it, the soda fountain was "a rendezvous for men whose wives fail to understand them." The *New York Times* stated authoritatively that the fountain man's prime requirement, "aside from the ability to break an egg with one hand and pull the proper faucets . . . is the ability to bandy words."

Almost as seamlessly as hotel bars became hotel fountain rooms, the Bartenders Union became the Drink Dispensers Union. The standards were high and a good dispenser could demand a salary almost as good as his boss. Ironically, the barmen from what the temperance movement dubbed the "antisocial saloon" helped make the fountain—once the spot for a quick fix—a genuine hangout.

This was the Jazz Age, ladies and gents. Gone were the days of staid socializing in the family parlor and courting on the front porch. In the modern era, nightlife was every bit the moneymaker that the working day once was. The terrible human toll of the Great War, as we called World War I in the post-war decade; the transformation of America into a country where more than half of the population was urban; the fast cash of a stock market that defied gravity—all gave rise to a jaded generation, jacked up on jazz and flush with disposable income. And you didn't have to be in Harlem or Chicago to hear the new tempo—the twenties roared a little louder all over the nation.

"Nobody stays at home anymore," noted author Willa Cather, the laureate of the prairie. Cather's fellow novelist John Dos Passos was putting his young strivers in the drugstore where "instead of supper they ate some more ice cream sodas." Women, in particular, had turned into night owls, as decorum faded in the bright light of "modernity" and all that the bold term implied. In 1920, women won the right to vote, but they celebrated with less civic exercises—it was the jitterbugging flapper, and not the earnest suffragette, that best embodied women's emancipation.

All of which is to say that if the fountain was to stay alive, it had to stay open. "These are restless times," noted the hawkers of Flexlume Electric Displays. "Downtown streets are crowded every evening and into the night. People must be amused and the fountain . . . will get their share of the amusement money." Hours grew later, menus grew longer, and smart proprietors put a Victrola phonograph on the counter right next to the state-of-the-art juice extractor—both these novelties helped draw a crowd.

Druggists sold phonographs and sheet music as side items early in the century, sometimes as premiums for purchases (so you could sing along with the Bromo-Seltzer Ta-Ra-Ra-Boom-De-Ay)

or as advertisement—the first pharmaceutical jingle if you will. But as the fountain established itself as a gathering place to rival the speakeasy, music graduated from the cash register to the counter. Ragtime records and player pianos were standard fare at a good fountain, but if a Jazz Age fountain proprietor really wanted to draw a crowd, he might invest in "the 'wireless craze' which at present is holding the attention of the country from coast to coast" or even in a dance floor. One particularly gung-ho fountain owner cleared out the back room of his Wheeling, West Virginia, establishment to make room for an orchestra. In doing so, the fountain made room for a whole new clientele: dance-hall patrons in search of music as well as a drink.

"Everybody likes music," read an advertisement in *Fountain and Candy Topics* in 1928. "Music makes people happy. Music urges them to dance and have a good time—to spend more money!" Holcomb & Hoke promised that 85 cents of every dollar invested in their Electromuse phonograph jukebox would be pure profit for the proprietor—more than $1,500 a year in "amusement money."

The soda fountain was enhanced immeasurably by the added ambiance of music in the Jazz Age. But jazz itself owes a debt or two to the fountain. Take the dandy ditty "The Drugstore Cabaret," with lyrics by the aptly named Albert Sweet, winking at the heavy burden of the fountain during Prohibition. "On the drugstore 'still' we're countin' . . . "

Or take the debut composition of a fifteen-year-old musical prodigy who also worked as a soda jerk at Washington, D.C.'s, Poodle Dog Café. When the regular Poodle Dog pianist got so drunk that he fell off the piano bench, the soda jerk jumped in and segued seamlessly into his own "Soda Fountain Rag."

The kid's name was Duke Ellington.

THE LILY CUP IS FAR NICER
THAN ANY OLD FASHIONED
GLASS OR ANY OTHER PAPER CUP
THE PUBLIC SERVICE CUP CO., BROOKLYN, N.Y.

When Prohibitionists gazed through their rose-colored glasses, they saw the ubiquitous fountain as a place where men would talk shop over buttermilk, progressive women could plot social reform with a side of soda, and tenement urchins would get their daily dose of nutrients in an ice cream cone. That happened for sure, in fountains from Fifth Avenue to Fargo. But what also happened was that the best laid plans of Prohibitionists tripped over the times. In one of the supreme ironies of history, the stern judges of the saloon had helped usher in the wildest party the country had ever seen. And it owed everything to Prohibition, which gave license to flaunt authority. The failure of the Volstead Act to banish alcohol abuse from American society is well documented. Some historians estimate that consumption of alcohol more than doubled during the dry years—and that rotgut, organized crime, and corruption was the most lasting legacy of the reformists' war on booze.

Naturally there was a backlash, one that would eventually result in a reversal of the Eighteenth Amendment and Prohibition's repeal. But first, the soda fountain felt the sting of suspicion. Prohibition, said temperance watchdogs, if not enforced stringently would facilitate the boozing up of the soda fountain. The Volstead Act had three exemption clauses: alcohol could be produced and distributed for sacramental purposes, for home consumption, and for medicinal purposes. The first two exemptions gave rise to a boom in Communion wine and bathtub gin, while the third resulted in a glut of licensed pharmacists. At least fifteen thousand of them applied for permits to supply so-called "whisky-medicines" within the first six months of the Volstead enactment. Plenty of others got into the game from the ground floor. Remember Jay Gatsby? Early in F. Scott Fitzgerald's classic Jazz Age novel, Gatsby's ditzy girlfriend attributes his newfound wealth to the fact that he "owns some drug-stores. A lot of drug-stores." In 1925, when

The Great Gatsby was published, the meaning of this venture, notes historian Daniel Okrent, "was clear as gin."

It wasn't just slick gents like Jay Gatsby who recognized opportunity in the Volstead's medicine clause to patent medicines of the nineteenth century, which prompted the American Medical Association to remove alcohol from the American Pharmacopoeia of acceptable medicines in 1916. Well, that didn't last. In 1922, the AMA reconsidered. The result, as Okrent puts it, "revealed an extraordinary coincidence: the booming prescription trade had been accompanied by a dawning realization . . . that alcoholic beverages were in fact useful in treating twenty-seven separate conditions including diabetes, cancer, asthma, snakebite, and old age."

In other words, the Volstead Act had opened the floodgates for unscrupulous soda men to adulterate their stock. The mayor of Buffalo, New York, sounded a typical paranoia when he claimed in 1923 that "hardware stores, drug stores, and grocery stores are . . . going into the soft drink business" as a way to sell booze outright or some dangerous substitute. He claimed that there were five thousand soft drink establishments in Buffalo, a city of five hundred thousand. In Butte, Montana, it was found that only thirty-two of the one hundred establishments selling soft drinks could be considered free of "potions [that] belie their titles." Spokane, Washington, gained sixty-five new drugstores within the first year of Prohibition; Chicago added seven thousand new soda fountains. (Yes—seven thousand!) Indicating just how far the fountain had fallen in the public trust, the city council of Aurora, Illinois, levied a ten dollar saloon ordinance in 1922 on all shops selling "pop, near beer, grape juice, and other carbonated beverages."

The witch hunt for soft drinks with "too much kick" wasn't always false accusation. In some respects, the outcry just picked up where the crusade against mystery patent medicines left off, with the

JOHN RUSSELL WARD AND
THE SODA FOUNTAIN (TRADE MAGAZINE)

Published monthly from 1897 to 1946, *The Soda Fountain* was the definitive resource for fountain operators, manufacturers, vendors, and staff. (Not to mention fountain historians!).

It was in the advertisements, letters, features, and classifieds of *The Soda Fountain* that we found the arc of our history (and our title as well!).

Too long muffled in his archives, we are pleased to reintroduce John Russell Ward, the journal's prolific and slightly pompous editor, as our favorite primary source.

On the qualities of a good soda dispenser:

" . . . should be friendly and interested in his customers without the obnoxious familiarity and 'freshness' which is seen so many times and which is more or less offensive than the double barreled 'grouch.' It is examples like this that keep bright the fires of optimism in the breasts of the observer of soda fountain observations . . . "

On the National Recovery Act during the Depression:

"Here is a wide open opportunity for retail soda fountains to put their shoulders under their share of the economic burden, thereby not only accomplishing an epochal act of rehabilitation at a time when it is most sorely needed, but benefiting—who shall say to what measure—on their own account."

On the merits of female soda jerks:

"If anybody thinks I am going to assume responsibility for the expression of Mr. Louis Spilman about [female] soda dispensers, he is giving me more credit than I posses."

On Prohibition and its enforcement:

"It is also true that the soda fountain has taken on an enormous momentum within the ten years or so in which prohibition has nominally been in operation but there are organic reasons entirely aside from any question of prohibition, even if the law were actually enforced, which, in spite of the fanciful claims of certain dry fanatics, is known to be farcical."

claim that "soft drink" was a code word for hard stuff in disguise. The same vanguards of temperance who had once upheld the attributes of soda as an antidote to alcohol were scrutinizing the fountain even before Prohibition was passed, searching for signs of sin. They found them. "The reformers are always with us," lamented the operator of one soda parlor. "When it isn't one bunch it's another." This particular complaint was leveled at the "doctors who see in the soda fountain the doom of the nation."

"What's in Coca-Cola?" asked the *Atlanta Constitution*. "Poison!" answered the *Pittsburgh Leader* definitively, which proudly led a "Crusade against Soft Drinks in Pennsylvania." Testifying against the pernicious influence of Coca-Cola, one evangelist preacher claimed the beverage had turned the nation's youth into "wild nocturnal freaks." The brewing industry joined the crusade in an eleventh hour attempt to save its own beer-making bacon. Soda went on the defensive, facing allegations from the Liquor Dealer's Benevolent Association that the fountain was no better than "the kindergarten . . . for the young women drunkards of the land."

Such was the contradictory public opinion of a century ago, when soda simultaneously represented both the antidote to alcohol's social scourge and the viper that slithered from the abandoned saloon. Almost certainly, some Prohibition era druggists allowed their medicine whiskies to spill into fountain drinks, but most soda men kept it clean for the sake of bigger gains. Jacob Baur of Liquid Carbonic urged his peers not to sully soda's reputation. He penned multiple opinion pieces and circulars warning that "antagonistic elements are endeavoring to undermine the sale of soda fountain beverages." "Depend upon it;" he thundered, "anyone who even whispers a word against the wholesomeness of soda water is willfully or thoughtlessly repeating a canard started for selfish business reasons."

Another soda pundit, Emile Hiss, advised, "Any dispenser who has a proper pride in his profession and a little ingenuity can fix up a drink which will look exactly like 'the real thing' without breaking any laws." In fact, a scrupulous pharmacist was an important source of law and order, suggested FBI director J. Edgar Hoover fifty years later. He is, he asserted, "A reliable citizen in a sea of unknown, a pillar of the community."

Prohibition had been good to the fountain: soda fountain receipts doubled, Coca-Cola sales tripled, and ice cream was gobbled with the avidity that allowed one fountain in Bridgeport, Illinois, to sell a "Goliath" soda, reputedly two feet tall. But like all good things, it did end. Anti-Prohibition sentiment, like the antialcohol movement that birthed it, was essentially a conservative social reaction. Dry crusaders of the nineteenth century railed against the disorder, abuse, and dereliction caused by drunken men. Wet crusaders of the twentieth pointed to bootlegging, organized crime, corrupt enforcement, and flagrant public drinking. They saw Prohibition as assurance that the youngest generation would be raised "with a total lack of respect for the Constitution and the law."

The dismantling of the Volstead Act began in February 1933, when Congress formally proposed the repeal of the Eighteenth Amendment. One month later, Franklin Delano Roosevelt was inaugurated as president, and on Repeal Day, December 5, 1933, he mixed himself a martini—the White House's first legal cocktail in over a decade. Tasked with repairing a collapsed banking system and runaway employment, he must have really needed it.

American Druggist

The Pharmac... ...usiness Paper

Founded in 1871

RCX   06977

August 1929
50 Cents

Robt. Robinson

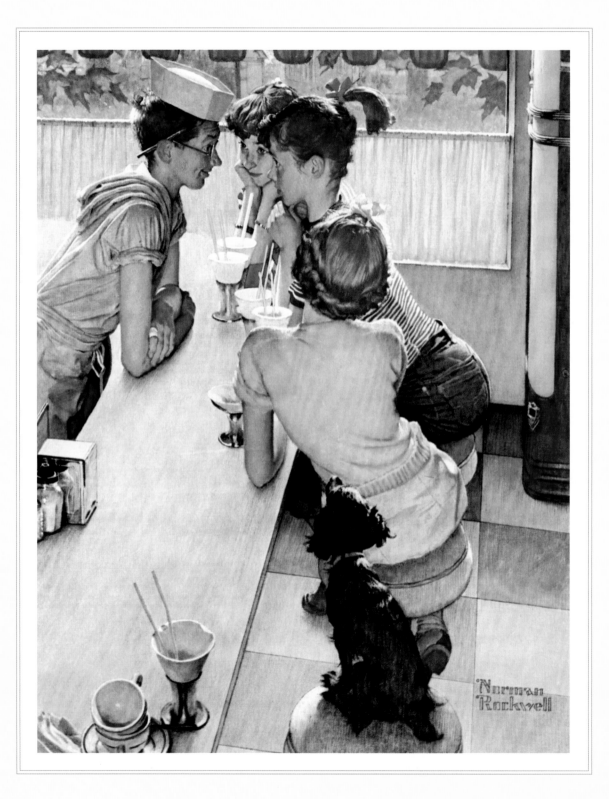

CHAPTER FOUR

STARS AND STRIPES (AND SODA) FOREVER

The dire economics of the Great Depression dictated the path for the soda fountain: it had to cut costs and it had to serve lunch. Some fountains had been doing so for a decade in order to better serve the saloon crowd. But in the 1930s, when so many customers stretched their dollar to fill their bellies, the five-cent soda and five-cent ice cream made way on the menu for the nickel hamburger. It was the fountain's next and final reinvention.

With nourishment a national pursuit, fountain owners stocked up on new ingredients: tomato malteds were pushed, sundaes were served on a bed of lettuce, a pamphlet full of artichoke dishes was a best-seller among fountain

owners, and yeast, that most basic alimentary building block, sneaked into myriad recipes. The nutritional value of ice cream and natural sugars were trumpeted as well. "Ice cream makes every meal a banquet of health," declared the National Dairy Council, and at least one fountain ran a campaign to sponsor a hungry child with a daily milkshake.

The transformation of the soda fountain from a watering hole to a culinary counter paved the way for the midcentury diners and luncheonettes that we still prize today as pure-blooded Americana. But the provision of wholesome economical fare at the fountain was an outcome of necessity—an entirely different purpose than that of the 1950s malt shop where kids threw their spending money and spoiled their dinners. In a fine piece of spin, one fountain booster praised the Depression-era counter as a place where "one does not ordinarily overeat."

Yes, milkshakes and malteds were mainstays, but during the bleakest years of the 1930s they might have come at the cost of hamburger, not as the accompaniment.

⸻

A cursory glance at soda fountain lunch favorites would not lead the modern diner to conclude that the fountain was all about "health food." Crabmeat and canned pineapple cocktail? Gelatin salad? Liver and onions on toast? Dubious. But in the 1930s, fountain owners started throwing out their stools, forcing patrons to eat and drink on the run. As a result, somebody back then even made the bold claim that the fountain is a place "where nutrition and physical fitness meet."

The removal of stools from the soda fountain counter was not done to keep diners fit and healthy. Rather, it was a recommendation from none other than Uncle Sam. This was the government's New Deal—to step into as many walks of American life as was necessary to provide relief. To employ millions struggling to feed their families, Washington ordered dams, highways, and hospitals. To send paychecks to unemployed writers and artists, FDR commissioned murals and travel guides. And for the bean counters, there were countless surveys to be executed. The Department of Commerce reviewed a quarter-million drug store transactions in the city of the St. Louis for the purpose of improving efficiency and profitability.

The results? A prototype Depression Counter—a forty-foot-long counter "scientifically altered past all recognition at a cost not exceeding $350." Now, whether or not their recommendations to lower the counter by a foot, remove outdated coffee urns, and clear a third of the bar of its stools constituted an alteration either "scientific" or "past all recognition," this new federal standard of counter efficiency was, if nothing else, an item of interest in that month's trade journals (and a paycheck for some well-fed surveyors in St. Louis).

With economy and efficiency directing the fountain's style, more and more businesses focused on take-out and even curbside service for the growing automobile trade. Owners and managers reevaluated the best payment system for luncheonette fountains—prepaid ticketing or postfare checks? Encourage quick turnover or suggest impulse buys? This is also the era that gave birth to a whole new language—the soda jerk lingo, which grew richer with time but almost always defied the notion of "shorthand." (Why was it quicker to say "bucket of black mud" than "chocolate soda"?)

Downtown fountain owners braced for the changing demands of their new breed of female patrons. Elbowing aside mothers and governesses were the stenographers with just twenty minutes for lunch. The fountain keeper's biggest complaint about this bunch was that "nine out of every ten who come up to the counter are chewing gum. And you can't chew gum and do justice to a ham sandwich or jelly roll at the same time." A common sign at the fountain lunch counter read "No Parking." It referred to the chewing gum cement accumulating on the underside of the counter.

Speaking of the modern gal—the twenties and thirties ushered in female dispensers, and with them, debate. Young women were steadily entering the workforce, often assisted by federal employment operations (like the one that installed one hundred waitresses at the Schrafft's luncheonettes in Philadelphia). There were plenty of complaints about this invasion of a traditionally all-male profession. One particularly put-out patron complained that "girls simply do not belong behind the soda fountain. I'm as sure of this as I am that Lindbergh can pilot an airplane." Centuries-old biases that women belong in the kitchen gave way to assertions that women can't be trusted behind the counter. You can probably almost hear them: "flighty," "flirty," "feeble," and so on. How dare they—right? (Then again, Lucille Ball was a fountain operator before she went on to be the most beloved bumbling beauty in the history of television. She was apparently fired for leaving the banana out of a banana split.) For the record, at Brooklyn Farmacy, we've been more than happy with our Jerkettes.

The lunch business, notwithstanding all its challenges, kept the fountain relevant and even critical to millions of loyal American patrons throughout the Great Depression. Sure, times were hard for fountains, too. Small-town druggists had to extend credit and accept chickens for payment. Big city operators postponed investments and lost margins to paper-slim profits. Job-wanted ads from "capable soda fountain executives" were plentiful. Manufacturers and suppliers took a

$40 million hit from the belt-tightening in the business. Still, the number of fountains grew . . . at a quarter the rate before the Depression, but growth nonetheless. In 1931, there were 110,000 fountains in the country—13,000 of them only a year old. Two years later, there were just as many still in operation, making $55,000 a year, according to *The Soda Fountain*, whose proud editor noted, "Any industry which can stand up under the strain of the past two years must be an essential industry or it would have gone down like jackstraws in a gale."

Many of those fountains were likely being run by new owners, it's true. In the first year of the Panic, when cash flow stopped and the economy was, in the evocative words of one historian, "a pool of glue," 28,000 small businesses went under. But the fountain was still a viable trade, taking strength in its own recovery efforts.

By 1933, the country was beginning its slow climb out of the Depression. Prosperity was still more than a decade away—and the nation would have to fight another world war to get there. But the worst of the slump was behind the soda fountain. The industry considered a "New Deal for Beverages" with the reintroduction of legal beer. Opinions varied on the pros and cons of freeing up counter space to serve beer along with soda, with the majority deciding to keep the fountain alcohol free. Meanwhile, the editor of *The Soda Fountain* exhorted fountain owners everywhere to embark on a soda fountain "national recovery act" by spending two hundred dollars each on postponed maintenances and fixture upgrades and thus bring the manufacturing business back from the brink.

Perhaps no better example of the resilience of the fountain during the Depression is Charles Walgreen, who opened his first drugstore fountain in 1893 on the sidelines of the Columbian Exposition in Chicago. In 1933, the Windy City was host to the World's Fair again. At the time, the city was hard-pressed to embody the fair's theme: "A Century of Progress," as one in three Chicagoans were out of work.

But Chicago prevailed, defying the bleakest projections for the fair's attendance and revenues. Charles Walgreen, who by then owned nearly five hundred stores employing twelve thousand workers, triumphed as the official pharmacy of the fair. His art-deco Marine Fountain, installed on the fairgrounds, was the world's largest, seating one hundred patrons at a time and boasting a hundred-foot-long aquarium behind the bar. His fountain brought in 4 percent of the Fair's gross profit. If 1933 was a low point in America's Century of Progress, it was still high ground for the soda fountain.

———

Hard times got easier, with the rigorous aid of the New Deal. But prosperity did not arrive until the United States agreed to go to war. World War II and the need to rearm a nation pulled the country from the grips of the Depression.

When American soldiers went to war following the attack on Pearl Harbor in 1941, soda and ice cream went with them. U.S. troops were the best-fed soldiers in the world, consuming an average of 4,758 calories—double that of the Japanese Imperial army. An astonishing amount of those calories came from ice cream. WWII food historian Lizzie Collingham estimates that the American GI consumed twenty-four ounces of milk a day, much of it in milkshakes. Soda fountain treats could be found on every American base and on more than a few aircraft carriers. The War Department listed confections, soft drinks, and ice cream as three indispensable items for troop morale.

Perhaps the most fervent wartime soda champion was General Dwight D. Eisenhower, who sent a stream of urgent cables to ensure a steady supply of the stuff. Three million bottles of Coke was insufficient, said Eisenhower, stationed in arid North Africa. He wanted front line factories

to keep those bottles filled and fizzy . . . and by George, he got it, along with 148 Coca-Cola Company bottling employees conscripted from the States to serve as technical observers for the United States Army.

If Coke won the war, ice cream helped win the victory. Both treats served GI Joe well in winning hearts and minds in occupied zones from the Philippines to France.

———

Back at home, a postwar economic boom was reshaping the soda fountain again.

Small druggists, forced to put their fountains on hold for the duration of the war, never brought them back. Instead, they made room to display the range of consumer products, from nylon pantyhose to glamour magazines, that symbolized a newly prosperous nation.

Chain drugstores kept the faith in the fountain. Statistics showed that overall sales for drugstores with fountains were 64 percent higher than those without. But with every reinvestment in those counters, came the need for uniformity and systematization. Embodied by automats, cafeterias, and franchised restaurants, self-service—a creative solution to the wartime shortage of employees—was yet another blow for a hand-drawn soda.

Social changes were no less significant than consumer trends. Americans in the 1950s moved to the suburbs and gathered in front of the TV with their take-home gallons of ice cream. Main Street began its slow decline. The supermarket swaggered. When families did go out to spend money, they

increasingly went in their car. Sometimes they never even left it as they slurped down a milkshake. Make no mistake—fast, tasty treats were still enshrined in the "American Way of Life." But in postwar America, indulgers were worshipping at the altars of the drive-in and the drive-through, of which there were forty thousand by 1961.

———

In 1969, the pharmacy on the corner of Henry and Sackett Street in Brooklyn closed its doors. That same year, the journal *Efficient Drug Store Management* had this to say about the old-fashioned soda fountain counter: "It should be thrown out."

By then, most of them had been.

The fountain as an apparatus for dispensing soda had gone full circle. From a simple spigot, to a countertop fancy, to a singular piece of furniture, to a whiz-bang operational bar, the soda fountain had, on the eve of disco, regressed into a utilitarian machine for fizzy beverages. It sat on a countertop. It was not pretty. It worked with the push of a button and minimal artistry, dispensing, at most, four name-brand soda giants.

We—you, me, our parents, and our kids—have imbibed millions of gallons of modern-day sodas from latter-day fountains. Sometimes, those sodas taste every bit as good as if they have been pulled from a tap and mixed with syrup before our eyes. Sometimes, they are not even close. Most often, we scarcely notice, busy as we are spilling ketchup over the armrest as we pass the fries to the back seat. Cue Joni Mitchell. We paved paradise and put up a Dairy Queen.

The introduction of food—indeed the supplanting of fizz by food—marked the beginning of the end of the soda fountain as an oasis strictly for imbibing. At the height of its necessity and at a moment when no one could imagine it being gone, it had already faded into a past glory. In 1946, *The Soda Fountain*, the stalwart journal that month after

month recorded changes, challenges, and news, changed the name of its publication. *The Soda Fountain* renamed itself *Fast Food*.

Postwar America embraced all that postwar prosperity offered: affordability, convenience, abundance, and ease. Soda had become all those things—available everywhere for the loose change in your pocket. From the Pacific Coast Highway to the Florida Bayou, Americans were confident that refreshment was readily available—perhaps from a roadside vending machine, perhaps from an ice chest in a corner store, or perhaps from a sliding glass window in the drive-through lane.

Rarely were they seeking refreshment from a soda fountain jerk.

A crying shame? Well yes, we think it was.

But it would take us a half century to realize what was lost when the soda fountain went franchised, burger-fied, and standardized. To miss what we had forgone: the artistry of creation, the magic of camaraderie, and the unique experience of watching a treat prepared before our eyes by a painstaking pro—a friendly one at that.

But here's the good news. America remembers. The soda fountain is a distant memory, but a powerful one. And it is bubbling back into our lives as surely as we write these lines. When The Farmacy opened its doors in June 2010, it was clear that we had tapped into a thirsty market. And not just for artisanal soda, but for the distinct fountain culture and the memories made at its counter, every day.

CHAPTER FIVE

A REVIVAL AT 513 HENRY STREET

Our building on the corner of Sackett and Henry is, like most of the mixed-use buildings of Carroll Gardens, about 130 years old. It's not as fancy as many of the elegant brownstones in the neighborhood. Its exterior is a brick mélange more reminiscent of the 1940s than the nineteenth century. It shares a block with establishments long in the tooth: Italian social clubs, a no-frills barber shop, a Chinese takeaway, and a pizza parlor that's been here forever. Brooklyn Farmacy is one of the newest kids on the block—but tell that to our fans who say walking into our place is like walking back in time.

For fifteen years before we moved into 513 Henry Street with our Bastian-Blessing soda fountain, the street-level corner was a curiosity. Always locked and clearly neglected, the space was in no way vacant. Passersby peeping through its dusty glass window could only wonder at the towering piles of boxes stacked along the walls, the lonely white pharmacist's coat hanging on a peg, and the unfamiliar

products lining the dusty shelves. The place was a neighborhood mystery.

Old-timers could still remember the Longos—the family who ran a pharmacy for two generations. They had a hazier memory of the eccentric who briefly opened his own drugstore before closing it in 1996. Others had a vague recollection of a failed market, back when a butcher sold meat and a baker sold bread and a merchant of urban organic products was an (unsuccessful) pioneer.

Peter Freeman moved into the apartment above the abandoned store in 2009. The neighborhood was in transition; Pete even more so. As Pete told his roommate, he was "seeking relevance."

One day while exploring the back stairway that led to the basement, he took a half-turn and opened up the door that led into the cluttered storefront. Filled to the rafters with a hundred years worth of history, the store was a time capsule—the resting place of ephemera from every decade since 1870.

Every decade, that is, except the last one. In the narrow pathway that led through the newspapers, mail, pharmaceutical products, medicine chests, and unopened bottles of Vermont maple syrup, Pete found his long-sought relevance. Because why should the rich history he was wading through stop now? Why shouldn't 513 Henry be a twenty-first century time capsule? A place where history was redolent, but not petrified.

And so Pete stopped being a squatter and started being a booster. He talked the owner, an introverted man who had turned down countless offers and ideas for the store, into giving him a key and permission to dream. Pete opened the front door and swept out the dust. The locals, who had stopped noticing the strange sight of an abandoned storefront on prime real estate, gathered, curious. Was something happening?

Pete did what he does best. He talked. He told them that the pharmacy was coming back, because

that's what this space always was and that's what it should still be. He said the Longos would probably still be in business if it weren't for one big mistake. "You mean Longo junior and the firearms racket he was running from the basement?" the wise guys cracked. "No," Pete would say. "Not that one. The fact that they never installed a soda fountain."

The plan was simple: to open a soda fountain and serve the best egg cream in Brooklyn. But it wasn't simple at all.

Pete spent the summer drawing a crowd to 513 Henry. There was a pig roast, a lobster fest. In retrospect, these were fund-raisers and media events, as well as good ways to leverage community support. But at the time, they were the only way Pete knew how to keep his dream afloat. They were rent parties—even if Pete still didn't have a lease.

By autumn, Pete had convinced much of the neighborhood of the merit of his project, but he was still at a standstill with the building's indecisive owner. He looked around the much-improved space and saw all the things he lacked. He needed design expertise; he needed an enthusiastic and reliable partner. He needed his sister, Gia. When he called and asked her to move to Brooklyn, Gia reminded him that she had just relocated her family to Israel. Pete did what Pete always does when confronted with an obstacle: he talked. Gia booked a flight the next day.

For the next three weeks, Pete and Gia spent every hour in the store. They cleaned, they rearranged, they listened to engineers and architects. They finally signed a lease and wrote a business plan. They tried not to think about the utter lack of funds they had to invest in that plan, focusing on the "cosmic" signals instead. One evening an old guy shuffled in off the street looking for castor oil.

Unfazed, Pete scanned the debris of his still clearly nonoperational establishment and spied an enormous jug of the stuff on a top shelf. It must have been forty years old, but the man said that was just what his aching joints needed.

That was the first and last "prescription" ever filled at Brooklyn Farmacy and that same old guy, "Sackett Street Joe," still comes by from time to time.

One morning Pete disappeared for the day. He returned that evening with a a spit-polished Bastian-Blessing soda fountain that he had found on eBay and picked up at a boy's detention center in Philadelphia. In 1952, it retailed for three thousand dollars. He paid four hundred dollars for it. A few days later, nine vintage fountain stools were located close enough to Brooklyn that Pete was able to pick them up and haul them back to the store.

And that was as far as the dream-happy siblings got when it came time for Gia to return to her family overseas: a soda fountain, a lease, and nine twirling bar stools. On the morning of Gia's flight, they were sitting on the bench outside the store. A kid on a scooter cruised past with his mother, who stopped to look in the window. Paying no mind to the uncharacteristically glum couple on the bench, the woman said to her son, "It looks like they're getting somewhere." And the kid, who didn't even need to turn his head to register the progress, said without the slightest doubt, "Yeah, that place is going to be great."

———

A month later, Gia got a phone call from her brother reporting that the pharmacy needed more than eighty thousand dollars worth of repairs in structural engineering alone. "If I really want to make egg creams," said Pete, "I should look for a job in Queens." It was his first admission of defeat.

That was Friday. On Sunday, Pete, still licking his wounds over the financial impossibilities, got

stood up by a date. "Whatcha gonna do?" he muttered. He threw open the door to the morning sunshine and grabbed the mop that for months had served as his motivation. He started to shine the penny tile floor. Outside, a car pulled up to the curb and a woman rolled down the window. She was lost. She needed directions. Pete started talking.

"Is this your store?" she asked, craning her neck. "Have you run into any construction problems?"

"Lady," said Pete, "you might want to turn off your car."

The woman, it turned out, was a casting director for a Discovery Channel television series called *Construction Intervention*. They were scouting properties for their season finale—which they hoped would be the story of a New York City small business dream that could only come true with the help of a fully funded miracle makeover.

A month later, a crew of sixty construction workers and designers, most of them Brooklynites, moved in. Gia and her family arrived around the same time, ready to make the neighborhood their new home. Over the course of four days, the *Construction Intervention* team did a complete renovation—mostly structural. On day five, Gia and Pete were ushered back into the soda fountain of their dreams. Half the neighborhood walked in with them.

We had done it. Not we, as in Pete and Gia. We, as in Pete, Gia, and all the soda fountain angels we never even knew were out there. Angels on skateboards with six-word blessings: "That place is gonna be great."

———

Brooklyn Farmacy & Soda Fountain opened its doors for business on June 6, 2010. From day one, we have been blessed with rave reviews and loyal customers. Our success has made something very clear—the thirst for what we are serving is deeper than we ever reckoned. This is a thirst not just for

our signature sundaes, it's a thirst for shared stories about the counters that have defined our life.

We did not invent the soda fountain, and we didn't open in a vacuum. We're one of at least one hundred working soda fountains across the country and the number is growing. We've been called, more than once, pioneers in a soda fountain revival. And while we certainly won't argue about the "pioneers" part (we've shed blood, sweat, and tears—isn't that what pioneers do?), we don't take the "revival" bit lightly. We know enough about the challenges of the business and the history of its rise and fall to bet on the future.

Here's what we do know: there is a revival happening at 513 Henry Street, and we'd like nothing more than to see it blossom beyond our counter. Here's to a new generation of soda fountains artists, starting with the "Jerk" holding this book.

CHAPTER SIX

GETTING STARTED

So you don't have a six-foot-long Bastian-Blessing soda fountain in your kitchen? No double well hot fudge dispenser? You haven't invested in a state-of-the-art three-spindle milkshake mixer?

Not to worry.

All of the recipes in the pages to come can be perfected in your own kitchen and served in your own dishes. The extent to which you want to replicate an old-fashioned soda fountain counter is up to you. Can't live without a bell glass for your egg cream? Search eBay and find just the thing. We have a Resources section at the back of the book that covers all of the items we suggest in this chapter, so you can kit out your kitchen to your heart's desire (see page 206).

Whether you plan to follow our step-by-step instructions precisely or prefer to embrace your inner jerk by experimenting, there are some fountain fundamentals we recommend you get under your belt before tackling the Flatbush Ave. float (page 98).

TOOLS AND RECOMMENDATIONS

While there is nothing wrong with giving your daily cereal bowls a welcome break from corn flakes, you can deck out your home fountain by scouring eBay and retro restaurant supply websites for vintage fountain glassware and equipment.

Once you're a pro, you can add a jaunty cap, a bow tie, and some red suspenders to complete your soda jerk style, but start with an apron. Ice cream can be messy. We recommend a bib apron, traditionally worn in old-fashioned soda fountains.

Get yourself two no-nonsense ice cream scoops: a small one (2 ounces) and a big one (4 ounces). We recommend Zeroll, a one-piece scoop with no moving parts. That way there's nothing to break when you go at some ice cream that hasn't fully thawed.

Ice cream dishes

You're gonna need them. Ain't no sundae that sits on a cone. For a full service counter, we recommend three basic vessels:

BEEHIVE SUNDAE BOWL: We recommend the Anchor Hocking 13-ounce footed dessert bowl, model number 513. We use this bowl for our larger sundaes.

TULIP SUNDAE DISH: We recommend a Libbey 6.25-ounce tulip sundae dish, model 5315 (pictured at right). We use this for our Anyday Sundae (page 111).

BANANA SPLIT BOAT: We use the Libbey 9-inch banana split dish, model 5317, but there are numerous dishes on the market to choose from.

Stainless steel sherbet dish

These are smaller, usually 5-ounce, and are ideal for making mini sundaes.

Fountain glass

For sodas, floats, and milkshakes, we recommend the Libbey model 5110, a 12-ounce, fluted tall glass on a short stem, a fountain classic.

Egg cream glass

We recommend the Anchor Hocking 12-ounce beverage glass, model 73012 (pictured below). If you're a traditionalist, you can scour the Internet for the old Libbey bell glass. They no longer mass-produce these, but if you're looking for them, they resemble old-fashioned Coca-Cola glasses. The fact is that thick-walled contemporary glasses are more durable, but if you are a historical stickler, knock yourself out! Just don't knock the bell glass. It will break!

:: **TIP** :: **KEEPING IT CHILL** :: The main thing to remember with your soda glasses is that the colder they are, the better they will help retain bubbles in your fizzy concoction. Keep your glasses chilled. Put them in the freezer for twenty minutes or fill them with ice water ten minutes before you intend to use them.

Jiggers

These are for measuring your soda syrups and are easily found in a bar supply or kitchenware store. We typically use two sizes, a 1-ounce and a 2-ounce.

Soda spoon
(also known as an iced tea spoon)

These extralong spoons allow you to reach to the bottom of a fountain glass.

Dessert plates

As we mentioned, ice cream is messy. We plate all of our ice cream scoops, sundaes, and floats. And not just to catch the overflow, but to enhance presentation, as well.

Whipped cream dispenser

At the Farmacy, we use a Whip-It professional cream whipper, a nitrous-oxide–charged whipped cream dispenser. Get one. You won't regret it. They come in all sizes and make fantastic whipped cream quickly, cleanly, and affordably. No beaters, no bowls of ice.

Straws

There are two types of straws we use at the soda fountain: soda straws and milkshake straws. Those most commonly found in the supermarket will be soda straws; whether straight or flexible, these are perfect for sipping sodas. Milkshake straws, sometimes called colossal straws, are wider, making thick milkshakes easier to drink. While these might be more difficult to locate in supermarkets, they are readily available online.

Attitude

The most powerful tool the soda jerk brings to the counter is creativity. Like the dispensers of the soda fountain's Golden Era, you, too, must have delight, flair, and panache in the practice of your craft to truly release your inner jerk.

CHAPTER SEVEN

SYRUPS & SODAS

Although fountain proprietors haven't actually used sodium bicarbonate to make water bubbly for nearly two hundred years, the term soda stuck around. It might be called *pop* in the Midwest or *soft drink* by your grandmother, or, in some circles, *club soda*. Here in Brooklyn, we're still hooked on *seltzer*. Whatever you call it, the key to good soda is high-quality syrups and ice-cold carbonated water. Because, as *The Soda Fountain* magazine informed fountain jerks in 1927, what the thirsty public wants is "bubbles out of their ears and eyes."

One of the earliest methods of creating bubbles in still water was to mix it with sodium bicarbonate. Even a century ago, the fashionable term for carbonated water was "mineral water," as that implied that the stuff was coming straight from the source, whether that was the springs of Vichy, Saratoga, Londonderry, or Ballston. The names were fancy; the minerals were basic: magnesium, potassium, strontium, and an inventory of salts. They all had different tastes and levels of effervescence.

Flavored fizzy water was a popular hit as early as 1830, when pharmacists regularly offered soda water laced with sweet syrups. More exotic additives were to be had as well, such as "Irish moss," a seaweed that produced a nice stable head (because you don't want a "windy soda" with too much foam) or coal tar for coloring.

So if you really want to impress your friends with an authentic old-fashioned soda order, come to The Farmacy and say: "I'll have a seaweed and coal tar soda, please." Who knows—it might make it onto our seasonal menu.

HOW TO MAKE A SODA

Making soda syrups, like everything at the fountain, is a process that entails loads of experimentation. But it always begins by laying in good-quality ingredients. That means buying spices from a reputable purveyor, selecting seasonal fruit for maximum flavor, and seeking out the odd ingredients that will bring out the essence of the syrup. The technique applied to the ingredients is equally important in assuring good flavor, so we spend a fair amount of time getting that right as well.

All of our recipes produce soda syrups of equal strength so that the instructions for mixing a soda are the same from one flavor to the next. To make a soda, fill a 12-ounce glass halfway with ice, add ¼ cup (2 ounces) of syrup, top with seltzer, and stir

gently with a soda spoon to combine. Of course, your own taste buds should ultimately determine how much syrup you use. Some want the punch of a powerful soda, while others prefer a "light" soda. At the fountain, we enjoy combining flavors as well. Some of our favorites are lemon-ginger, hibiscus-lime, cherry-cola, orange–vanilla cream, and pineapple-raspberry. Most of all, remember: It's not rocket science, it's soda science. Experiment!

:: TIP :: All of our recipes call for the use of regular granulated cane sugar because we feel it makes a better soda syrup. Sugar made from sugar beets is what's often sold in the center of the country, especially the Midwest. Beet sugar and cane sugar are both comprised of 99.95 percent sucrose. That .05 percent, made up of differences in trace minerals and proteins, is what sets the two so far apart. Some mass market brands of sugar are cane-based and that fact is usually trumpeted on their packages. What we use at the Farmacy is an even less processed cane sugar that's beige colored. With a little help from the Internet, you should be able to get your hands on some cane sugar in your local supermarket or health food store. Brands to look for include Florida Crystals, Wholesome Sweeteners, and Zulka. (See the Resources, page 206, for more information.)

We make over a dozen different syrups in our Farmacy kitchen, covering the standards and honoring the seasons. And while most of our syrups have been crowd-pleasers, we have not always succeeded: a really "peachy" peach syrup has thus far eluded us, orgeat was a painstaking pain-in-the-neck, and we're still fumbling about with apples. The quest, however, is exceptionally fun and a reward of its own kind. With that in mind, we invite you to try our recipes and wholeheartedly encourage you to embark on your own syrup quests.

SYRUP QUANTITIES AND STORAGE

For the most part, the recipes in this chapter make 4 cups of syrup, enough for 16 sodas. That may seem like a lot, but we figure that you'll want substantial results for the effort you've expended. And, we want to encourage you to share. (Go ahead, give the neighbor kid who mows your lawn a homemade lime soda. Impress your mother-in-law by serving her a ruby-hued hibiscus soda. Kiss up to your boss by giving him a bottle of ginger syrup.) Besides, the high sugar content in soda syrups means that they keep really well. Most can be stored for a few weeks in the refrigerator and many can be frozen to extend storage time to three months.

:: TIP :: You'll note that some of our syrup recipes call for citric acid. Sometimes labeled "sour salt," it may be found in most large supermarkets or health food stores, though you may need to ask where it's located in the store. Citric acid, naturally occurring in many fruits, is what gives lemons and limes their sour flavor. We use citric acid to impart tanginess without adding another flavor dimension.

TOOLS

Microplane zester for citrus

Fine and medium mesh strainers

Cheesecloth

Spice/coffee grinder
(to grind whole spices)

SELTZER

While the notion of a guy driving around in a truck delivering wooden crates filled with beautifully colored glass bottles of seltzer is romantic and nostalgic, it's not the reality today. Most folks buy their seltzer at the supermarket and a growing number of people make their own with a SodaStream, an easy-to-use home soda maker. If you're buying seltzer at the supermarket, pick up 1-liter bottles since they'll get used up more quickly, thus ensuring maximum fizziness. For use with our recipes, buy plain seltzer, not flavored. Always chill seltzer well before using it to make sodas, egg creams, or floats. If you're using a SodaStream, chill the flat water in the provided bottle before carbonating it: really cold water retains carbonation best. It can't be stressed enough how important cold seltzer is to the character of the bubbly drinks we serve at the fountain, and that you'll be serving at home.

VANILLA CREAM SYRUP

It's a mystery as to how cream soda evolved into what we know it as today. The earliest known recipe, published in 1852 in *Michigan Farmer*, did contain milk as well as a handful of other ingredients including cream of tartar, Epsom salts, and eggs. (Yum.) Flavorings such as vanilla, lemon, and lime were added to later versions, but at some point dairy was dropped from the ingredients and vanilla became the flavor most associated with cream soda.

Vanilla beans are far easier for the home cook to buy now than they once were. Many of the ones you'll find for purchase are from Madagascar, but they are grown the world 'round in immediate proximity to the equator. Where they come from (Uganda, India, Indonesia, and Mexico to name a few places) and how they are treated once picked from the vine greatly affect their scent and flavor. Try this recipe with vanilla beans from different places and you will taste for yourself. This syrup is featured in The Joey float (page 91).

3 cups (24 ounces) water

2¼ cups (18 ounces) cane sugar

¾ cup (5.3 ounces) firmly packed light brown sugar

¼ teaspoon citric acid

2 vanilla beans

3½ teaspoons pure vanilla extract

Put the 3 cups water, cane and brown sugars, and citric acid in a saucepan and bring to a boil over medium heat. Decrease the heat and simmer, covered, for 10 minutes. Remove from the heat, add the vanilla beans, and let steep, covered, for 1 hour. Let cool to room temperature and chill before using, keeping the vanilla beans in the syrup.

Store the syrup in covered glass jars or plastic containers in the refrigerator for up to 3 weeks. You may remove the vanilla beans from the syrup before storing; however, they continue to impart flavor so we recommend leaving them in.

To make a vanilla cream soda, fill a 12-ounce glass halfway with ice, add ¼ cup (2 ounces) of Vanilla Cream Syrup, top with seltzer, and stir gently with a soda spoon to combine.

CHERRY SYRUP

MAKES 3⅓ CUPS

Though it contains no fresh fruit, we engineered this syrup to taste the way we thought it should. If you want to use all-natural (yes, even the color!) maraschino cherries, buy Tillen Farms Merry Maraschinos. Merry Maraschinos, tart cherry juice concentrate, and Fox's U-Bet Vanilla Syrup can all be purchased online (see Resources, page 206). This syrup is featured in the Cherry Lime Rickey (opposite) and the Tootsie float (page 89).

2 cups (16 ounces) maraschino cherry "juice," strained from a jar of maraschino cherries (or see recipe, following)

1 cup (8 ounces) tart cherry juice concentrate (preferably from Montmorency cherries)

⅓ cup (2.6 ounces) Fox's U-Bet Vanilla Syrup

In a large bowl, combine all the ingredients and mix well. Chill before serving. Store the syrup in covered glass jars or plastic containers in the refrigerator for up to 2 weeks. The syrup may also be frozen in plastic containers for up to 3 months. If frozen, allow to thaw in the refrigerator overnight before using.

To make a cherry soda, fill a 12-ounce glass halfway with ice, add ¼ cup (2 ounces) of Cherry Syrup, top with seltzer, and stir gently with a soda spoon to combine.

MARASCHINO CHERRY "JUICE"

MAKES 2 CUPS

1⅓ cups (10.6 ounces) water

1⅓ cups (10.6 ounces) cane sugar

1¾ cups (11.6 ounces) maraschino cherries, finely chopped

To make a simple syrup, put the water in a saucepan and pour the sugar into the water. Over medium heat, bring the mixture to a simmer, stirring gently from time to time to release any sugar that may be stuck to the bottom of the pan. Cook until the sugar has dissolved, about 10 minutes. Remove from the heat and let the syrup cool to room temperature. Stir in the cherries, transfer to a bowl, cover, and let the mixture marinate for 12 hours in the refrigerator. Strain the mixture into another bowl, using a wooden spoon to press the solids against the mesh of the strainer to extract all the juices. Discard the solids that remain in the strainer.

Store the syrup in covered glass jars or plastic containers in the refrigerator for up to 2 weeks. The syrup may also be frozen in plastic containers for up to 3 months. If frozen, allow to thaw in the refrigerator overnight before using.

THE CHERRY LIME RICKEY

Rickeys had already been around for more than five decades when Glenn Miller's Orchestra recorded "Jukebox Saturday Night" in the early 1940s. They originated as a boozy concoction of whiskey, lime juice, and soda water. In the 1880s, Colonel Joe Rickey, a gambling man, Democratic lobbyist, and Confederate army veteran, purportedly instructed bartenders in the assembly of his favorite cocktail wherever he went and his signature drink came to be known as a "Joe Rickey." By the time F. Scott Fitzgerald wrote about them in *The Great Gatsby*, the whiskey in rickeys had been replaced by gin, which is how rickeys are still served today. And at some point a leap was made to booze-free rickeys, though the key ingredients have remained the same throughout the years: fresh lime juice and carbonated water.

To make a Cherry Lime Rickey, fill a 12-ounce glass halfway with ice, add 1 tablespoon (0.5 ounces) of Cherry Syrup (opposite) and 3 tablespoons (1.5 ounces) Lime Syrup (page 71). Top with seltzer and stir gently with a soda spoon to combine. Use a spoon to remove a maraschino cherry, along with some of the juice, from a jar of maraschinos and stir gently into the drink.

SODA FOUNTAIN LINGO

Soda fountain lingo and its sister tongue, diner jargon, are pretty much extinct languages these days. Even at Brooklyn Farmacy, where old-time is our idea of a good time, we don't relay orders for "Chicago with a side of balloon water" or a "leg off a pair of drawers." But we're perfectly aware that no history of the soda fountain is complete without a sampling of some of the terminology that was the native language of generations of jerks. A few favorites:

"Sweet Alice"... milk

"Armoured Cow"... canned milk

"Adam's Ale"... water

"City juice"... water

"Belch water"... seltzer water

"Balloon juice"... seltzer water

"Boulevard"... ice cream soda

"Belly chokers"... doughnuts

"Throw it in the mud"... add chocolate syrup

"Family reunion"... chicken and egg sandwich

"Twist it, choke it, and make it cackle"... a chocolate malt with egg

"Burn one"... chocolate malted milk

"Huddle soda"... one soda with two straws

"Let it walk"... order to go

"Leg off a pair of drawers"... pour a cup of coffee

COFFEE SYRUP

Please note that the coffee extract needs to "brew" in the refrigerator for 12 hours before you can make the coffee syrup. While a dark roast coffee is preferred in this recipe, any kind may be used, even decaf. This syrup is featured in the Coffee Egg Cream (page 106) and the Wake-Up Call float (page 93).

3 cups (7.5 ounces) dark roast coffee beans, coarsely ground

3¾ cups (30 ounces) cold water

2⅔ cups (21.4 ounces) cane sugar

¼ teaspoon citric acid

Combine the coffee and water in a large glass jar or bowl. Stir, cover tightly, and refrigerate for at least 12 hours. Remove from the refrigerator and set a strainer, lined with a paper towel, over a large bowl or container. Pour the coffee mixture, in small manageable batches, into the strainer, allowing the liquid to drain completely from the solids and changing the paper towel for each batch. (This will take some time as you want to capture all the coffee extract you can.) This should make about 2¼ cups of coffee extract.

Combine the coffee extract, sugar, and citric acid in a medium saucepan. Cook over medium heat, stirring occasionally, until the sugar has dissolved, about 10 minutes. Remove from the heat and let cool to room temperature.

Chill before serving. Store the syrup covered glass jars or plastic containers in the refrigerator for up to 3 weeks.

To make a coffee soda, fill a 12-ounce glass halfway with ice, add ¼ cup (2 ounces) of Coffee Syrup, top with seltzer, and stir gently with a soda spoon to combine.

LEGENDS OF THE SODA FOUNTAIN:
HARRY SOLOMON DOLOWICH

New York during Prohibition was a city run by the rackets. Every business, no matter how niche, was a potential source of revenue to the opportunistic eye. There was a milk racket. Also, a kosher chicken racket, a furrier "association," and a mini-golf mob. In fact, mobsters had laid claim to over three hundred niche businesses in commercial New York by 1930—and one of them was the soda syrup business.

Harry Solomon Dolowich was a son of the Lower East Side tenements. His schemes to "make good" involved squeezing local syrup makers for a piece of their profits. His story is a fascinating glimpse at the sometimes sticky business of soda making.

Dolowich grew up on Delancey Street near the Lefkowitz & Son soda syrup factory. He got a degree from Brooklyn Law School and promptly put it to use to "organize" the city's syrup manufacturers, starting with Lefkowitz himself. Joining his "association," he promised, was a cakewalk to bigger profits. Lefkowitz and many others signed up. They paid a two hundred dollar initiation fee and six dollars per week per truck thereafter. Further fines and payments were levied as necessary until Dolowich had a new Studebaker and a fancy apartment on Manhattan's Riverside Drive. Food historian Andrew Coe reckons he controlled well over half the city's syrup, but a few operators balked. When they did, says Coe, Dolowich gave them a new offer: "join or be ruined."

Almost as quick as he got rich, Dolowich was laid low. The good guys, in this case, won. After three years of intimidation and collusion, syrup vendors Samuel Snaider, Rebecca Kaplan, Isidore Trachtenberg, and Leon Rakowsky, took their complaints to the Deputy Attorney General and the racket was broken up. Dolowich was sentenced to Welfare Island penitentiary in February 1932. His three-year reign as soda syrup czar was over. No one inherited Dolowich's take. The soda industry was free again.

COLA SYRUP

MAKES 2½ CUPS

Yes, the ingredients list here is as long as your arm, but the results are worth the effort. You can also double or triple the recipe if you're so inclined since this syrup keeps well. Vanilla bean paste is becoming easier to find as its admirers grow in number. Look for it online or in a gourmet or natural food store with a comprehensive herb and spice section. The caramel color, which can be found online, is completely optional. We've added it to this recipe to make the syrup a darker shade of brown, but it doesn't alter the flavor in any way. A food processor or a powerful blender is helpful to break down the sugars so they dissolve more easily. This syrup is featured in the Choco-Cola float (page 86).

2 cups (16 ounces) water

Freshly grated zest from 2 medium oranges

Freshly grated zest from 2 medium limes

Freshly grated zest from 1 medium lemon

½ teaspoon dried lavender flowers

¼ teaspoon freshly grated nutmeg

⅛ teaspoon ground cinnamon

¼ teaspoon citric acid

½ teaspoon vanilla bean paste

1 section of a star anise pod, crushed

1 tablespoon peeled and finely chopped fresh ginger

1¾ cups plus 2 tablespoons (15 ounces) cane sugar

1 tablespoon (0.4 ounces) firmly packed light brown sugar

¾ teaspoon caramel color (optional)

Put the water, citrus zests, lavender, nutmeg, cinnamon, citric acid, vanilla paste, star anise, and ginger in a saucepan and bring to a boil over medium heat. Decrease the heat and simmer, covered, for 20 minutes.

While the aromatics are simmering, put the cane and brown sugars and caramel color in a blender or in the work bowl of a food processor fitted with a steel blade and run for 30 seconds. Empty the mixture into a large, heatproof bowl. Line a strainer with a double layer of cheesecloth and set it over the bowl of sugar.

Remove the aromatics from the heat and immediately pour them through the cheesecloth. When cool enough to handle, but while the syrup is still hot, gather up the corners of the cheesecloth and twist at the top to form a small bundle. Press on it with the back of a wooden spoon against the mesh of the strainer to extract all the liquid it still retains. Discard the bundle, remove the strainer, and stir the syrup briefly to help dissolve the sugar. Stir occasionally until all the sugar has dissolved. Let the syrup cool to room temperature, and chill before using.

Store the syrup in covered glass jars or plastic containers in the refrigerator for up to 3 weeks.

To make a cola soda, fill a 12-ounce glass halfway with ice, add ¼ cup (2 ounces) of Cola Syrup, top with seltzer, and stir gently with a soda spoon to combine.

BLUEBERRY SYRUP

We wait for the arrival of blueberry season (always around July 4 in the Northeast) the way a dog waits for a bone: not very patiently. Blueberry Syrup can be used to make sodas, floats, lemonade, and egg creams. Unlike many of the other fruit syrups we make, this syrup has a particular affinity for milk and when combined with seltzer, the ingredients come together to make a delicious egg cream that is a beguiling shade of lavender. Speaking of lavender, you need not buy dried lavender flowers if you know someone who's growing it pesticide free. If you do need to buy it, try a gourmet or natural foods market with a comprehensive herb and spice section. This syrup is featured in the Blueberry Egg Cream (page 107), Purple Haze float (page 91), and Rhapsody in Blue float (page 92).

2 pints fresh blueberries, or 24 ounces frozen blueberries

3 cups (24 ounces) cane sugar

¼ teaspoon dried lavender flowers

1 tablespoon freshly squeezed lemon juice

¾ cup water

Put the blueberries, sugar, and lavender in a saucepan. Stir briskly, mashing a few blueberries in the process. Cover and let sit at room temperature for 30 minutes. Add the lemon juice and water and bring to a boil over medium heat, stirring occasionally. Decrease the heat and let simmer, uncovered, for 15 minutes.

Place a fine-meshed strainer over a bowl and pour the berry mixture into it in manageable batches, using a wooden spoon to mash the mixture against the mesh of the strainer. Discard the mash that remains in the strainer (although it would probably taste pretty darn good over vanilla ice cream or pound cake.) Let the syrup cool to room temperature and chill before using.

Store the syrup in covered glass jars or plastic containers in the refrigerator for up to 2 weeks. The syrup may also be frozen in plastic containers for up to 3 months. If frozen, allow to thaw in the refrigerator overnight before using.

To make a blueberry soda, fill a 12-ounce glass halfway with ice, add ¼ cup (2 ounces) of Blueberry Syrup, top with seltzer, and stir gently with a soda spoon to combine.

GINGER SYRUP

Unlike most other sodas, the histories of which are inextricably tied to America, ginger-flavored sodas originated in England in the mid-eighteenth century. (It was brewed ginger beer that was popular then, as opposed to the ginger ale that we are more accustomed to now.) The incisive and spicy flavor of ginger is very volatile and degrades quickly, so use this syrup shortly after making it. This syrup is featured in the KiKi float (page 92) and the Hey, Pumpkin! float (page 86).

2 cups (8 ounces) unpeeled, washed, coarsely chopped fresh ginger

2 cups (16 ounces) cane sugar

3 cups (24 ounces) water

1 by 1-inch piece washed and unpeeled piece fresh ginger

Put the 2 cups chopped ginger, sugar, and the 3 cups water in a saucepan and bring to a boil over medium heat. Decrease the heat and simmer, covered, for 1 hour. Remove from the heat and pour through a strainer set over a bowl, pressing on the solids with the back of a wooden spoon to extract all the liquid they still retain. Discard the contents of the strainer and let the syrup cool to room temperature.

Grate the 1 by 1-inch piece of ginger into a small strainer set over a glass or mug. Press the solids against the mesh of the strainer with the back of a teaspoon to extract all the juice they still retain. Add 1 teaspoon of the ginger juice (or more if your taste buds demand it) to the cooled ginger syrup and stir. Chill before using.

Store the syrup in covered glass jars or plastic containers in the refrigerator for up to a week.

To make a ginger soda, fill a 12-ounce glass halfway with ice, add ¼ cup (2 ounces) of Ginger Syrup, top with seltzer, and stir gently with a soda spoon to combine.

PINK GRAPEFRUIT SYRUP

MAKES 4 CUPS

This recipe requires 1½ cups of freshly squeezed grapefruit juice, which you should be able to get from two grapefruits. If your grapefruits are not particularly juicy, you may need more than two. Both dried hibiscus flowers and orange flower water may be found online. If you're looking to find either one at a brick-and-mortar store, it helps to know that hibiscus is used predominantly in the Caribbean and Mexico and orange flower water is prevalent in the Middle East. This syrup is featured in the Let's Head South float (page 96).

2 medium pink or red grapefruit

1¼ cups (10 ounces) water

2 cups plus 2 tablespoons (17 ounces) cane sugar

¼ cup (0.4 ounce) dried hibiscus flowers, tied in a cheesecloth sack (optional)

1¼ teaspoons freshly squeezed lemon juice

¼ teaspoon orange flower water (optional)

Wash the grapefruits, zest 1 of them, then juice both. Set the zest and juice aside separately.

Put the 1¼ cups water in a saucepan and pour the sugar into the water. Bring to a boil over medium heat, stirring gently from time to time to release any sugar that may be stuck to the bottom of the pan. Cook until the sugar has dissolved, about 10 minutes. Remove from the heat and add the grapefruit zest and the bundle of dried hibiscus blossoms to the syrup. Let steep, covered, for 10 minutes. Remove the bundle and squeeze it over the saucepan to extract any liquid it still retains. Discard the bundle and let the simple syrup cool to room temperature.

Add 1½ cups of the grapefruit juice, the lemon juice, and orange flower water to the cooled simple syrup and stir. Chill before using.

Store the syrup in covered glass jars or plastic containers in the refrigerator for up to 2 weeks. The syrup may also be frozen in plastic containers for up to 3 months. If frozen, allow to thaw in the refrigerator overnight before using.

To make a pink grapefruit soda, fill a 12-ounce glass halfway with ice, add ¼ cup (2 ounces) of Pink Grapefruit Syrup, top with seltzer, and stir gently with a soda spoon to combine.

HIBISCUS SYRUP

Tart and sweet and a brilliant ruby color, hibiscus soda will quench your thirst even on the hottest summer days. It's no wonder then that dried hibiscus flowers can be found most easily in markets catering to customers from warmer climes, such as Mexico, Jamaica, and the Caribbean. Some larger health food stores may also carry dried hibiscus flowers. This syrup is featured in the Pink Poodle float (page 97).

2⅔ cups (21.4 ounces) water

2⅓ cups (18.6 ounces) cane sugar

⅔ cup (1 ounce) dried hibiscus flowers

2 tablespoons plus 2 teaspoons freshly squeezed lemon juice

Put the 2⅔ cups water in a saucepan and pour the sugar into the water. Bring to a boil over medium heat, stirring gently from time to time to release any sugar that may be stuck to the bottom of the pan. Cook until the sugar has dissolved, about 10 minutes. Remove from heat and stir in the hibiscus flowers. Let steep, covered, for 30 minutes. Pour through a strainer set over a bowl, pressing on the solids with the back of a wooden spoon to extract all the liquid they still retain. Discard the contents of the strainer and let the syrup cool to room temperature. Add the lemon juice and stir. Chill before using.

Store the syrup in covered glass jars or plastic containers in the refrigerator for up to 3 weeks. The syrup may also be frozen in plastic containers for up to 3 months. If frozen, allow to thaw in the refrigerator overnight before using.

To make a hibiscus soda, fill a 12-ounce glass halfway with ice, add ¼ cup (2 ounces) of Hibiscus Syrup, top with seltzer, and stir gently with a soda spoon to combine.

THE HAZARDS OF THE TRADE

Carbonic acid, the necessary ingredient for making fizzy water fizz, is a none-too-innocent element. Explosions were common in the cellars and back rooms where early soda manufacturers worked out the kinks in a highly combustible algorithm of gas and pressure. Calamities were not unheard of, even after Jacob Baur did soda men everywhere a favor by figuring out how to contain the explosive gas in a cylinder for easy use.

From the *New York Times*, July 1895
"Hudson Mass. Five soda cylinders charged with carbonic acid gas, which were lying in the yard back of Seymore's Block, exploded this afternoon. They were the property of T.F. Mahoney. Pieces were blown to a height of 100 feet, coming down from 400 to 500 feet from their starting point."

From a report of the Chief Inspector of the Bureau for the Safe Transportation of Explosives and Other Dangerous Articles, 1912
"About 4 a.m. a truckman . . . loaded 6 cylinders on a warehouse truck, and upon reaching the end of the transfers one of the cylinders exploded, resulting in his death."

From *The Soda Fountain*, February 1922
Plate glass windows were hurled into the street, soda water and ice cream scattered in all directions and residents of Winchester, Mass., were startled today when a cylinder of carbonic gas in the Arnold Colgate Ice Cream Company at No. 420 Main street, in that city, exploded.

From *The Soda Fountain*, February 1923
"Explosion lifts soda store in Louisville Kentucky off its foundations."

DRINKS FOR DISAPPOINTED MEN

G. K. Chesterton spoke for an aggrieved generation when he resigned himself to "silly drinks that fill you up with gas and self righteousness" during Prohibition. Soda fountain owners were advised to cater to millions in search of a manly drink and quiet watering hole. The trick was to employ a nice-looking lady jerk. But that would only go so far: "You'll have to reach him through his thirst, not his eyes," warned *The Soda Fountain* trade journal.

Still and all, some men were not to be brought around to the mixed company of the soda fountain counter. United Candy Stores opened a fountain for men only in 1923, promising "a real man's fountain with brass rails, hard boiled eggs, and free pretzels." This resulted in drinks for a new breed of soda patron, such as the John Collins, which *The Soda Fountain* described as "first cousin of the late lamented Tom."

LEMON SYRUP

MAKES 4 CUPS

This is a very versatile syrup that blends well with most other flavors of syrups and can be used as a base for making lemonade. Sixteen medium lemons should yield you 2 cups of lemon juice. Make sure to zest three of the lemons before juicing them all! This syrup is featured in the Dalmatian float (page 87).

1 cup (8 ounces) water

2⅔ cups (21.4 ounces) cane sugar

Freshly grated zest from 3 medium lemons

2 cups (16 ounces) freshly squeezed lemon juice

Put the 1 cup water in a saucepan and pour the sugar into the water. Bring to a boil over medium heat, stirring gently from time to time to release any sugar that may be stuck to the bottom of the pan. Cook until the sugar has dissolved, about 10 minutes. Remove from the heat and add the zest. Let the syrup cool to room temperature. Add the juice and stir. Chill before using.

Store the syrup in covered glass jars or plastic containers in the refrigerator for up to 3 weeks. The syrup may also be frozen in plastic containers for up to 3 months. If frozen, allow to thaw in the refrigerator overnight before using.

To make a lemon soda, fill a 12-ounce glass halfway with ice, add ¼ cup (2 ounces) of Lemon Syrup, top with seltzer, and stir gently with a soda spoon to combine. To make lemonade, follow the directions for making a lemon soda, substituting flat water for the seltzer.

LIME SYRUP

MAKES 4 CUPS

Sixteen medium limes should yield you 2 cups of lime juice, but buy some extra because limes can vary wildly in the amount of juice they yield. This syrup is featured in the Tarty Pants float (page 87).

1 cup (8 ounces) water

2⅔ cups (21.4 ounces) cane sugar

Freshly grated zest from 8 medium limes

2 cups (16 ounces) freshly squeezed lime juice

Follow the instructions for lemon syrup, above.

To make a lime soda, follow the instructions above.

NEW ORLEANS MEAD SYRUP

MAKES 5 CUPS

In the heyday of the American soda fountain, varying recipes for root beer abounded and were well-guarded by those who made them. New Orleans mead was another (and far sexier) name for root beer. While the nomenclature and ingredient lists varied greatly, the common denominator was sassafras root, which gives root beer its defining flavor. Native Americans used sassafras for medicinal purposes and the English settlers of Jamestown, Virginia adopted its use for that reason, but also because sassafras wood was lovely and durable. For a brief period of time in the seventeenth century, sassafras was the second most important export from America after tobacco.

In 1960, the FDA curtailed the use of sassafras root because the oil it produced, safrole, was deemed carcinogenic. Most root beers now contain synthesized versions of sassafras, but safrole-free sassafras extracts can be located online if you're looking for them. For our recipe, we opted to use a product called Pappy's Sassafras Concentrate Instant Tea, which we found on Amazon. Whole spices are called for in this recipe because they'll impart the most vibrant flavor. Use a spice or coffee grinder to grind them. Whole nutmegs are particularly tough to break down. Smashing is the best way: put the nutmeg on a wooden cutting board and firmly, but carefully, smash it with the bottom of a cast-iron skillet or other suitably heavy-duty pan. This syrup is featured in the Gosh Nog It! float (page 97).

1½ teaspoons whole cloves

1½ teaspoons whole allspice

1 (1½-inch) section of a cinnamon stick

½ smashed nutmeg

1½ teaspoons ground mace

1½ teaspoons peeled and finely chopped fresh ginger

¼ teaspoon vanilla bean paste

4 cups (32 ounces) water

2⅔ cups (21.4 ounces) cane sugar

6 tablespoons (4.5 ounces) honey

5 tablespoons (2.5 ounces) Pappy's Sassafras Concentrate Instant Tea

Put the cloves, allspice, and cinnamon stick in a spice or coffee grinder and grind for 10 to 15 seconds. Put the ground cloves, allspice, cinnamon, nutmeg, mace, fresh ginger, vanilla, the 4 cups water, and sugar in a saucepan and bring to a boil over medium heat. Decrease the heat and simmer, covered, for 1 hour.

Line a strainer with a double layer of cheesecloth and set it over a bowl. Remove the aromatics from the heat and immediately pour the mixture through the cheesecloth. When cool enough to handle, but while the syrup is still hot, gather up the corners of the cheesecloth and twist at the top to form a small bundle. Press on it with the back of a wooden spoon against the mesh of the strainer to extract all the liquid it still retains. Discard the bundle and remove the strainer. Add the honey and sassafras concentrate to the spice mixture and stir to combine. Let the syrup cool to room temperature and chill before using.

Store the syrup in covered glass jars or plastic containers in the refrigerator for up to 3 weeks.

To make a New Orleans mead soda, fill a 12-ounce glass halfway with ice, add ¼ cup (2 ounces) of New Orleans Mead Syrup, top with seltzer, and stir gently with a soda spoon to combine.

ORANGE SYRUP

Though orange syrup is not an uncommon soda fountain flavor, our version has serendipity to thank for its deliciousness. After we opened in 2010 and sweated through our first summer, the harvest-time bounty dried up and by late November we were scratching our heads wondering what kind of seasonal fruit syrup we could make next. That's when an email arrived in our inbox advertising combination boxes of navel and Page oranges from The Orange Shop in Citra, Florida. Page oranges were wholly unknown to us, but a little research into their provenance led us to believe they'd be great in combination with straight-up navels or Valencia oranges.

A cross between the Minneola tangelo and clementine mandarin, Page oranges (not really oranges after all, but three-fourths tangerine and one-fourth grapefruit) were introduced in 1942. Despite their exquisite flavor, they didn't do well commercially and faded into obscurity. Pete and Cindy Spyke, owners of The Orange Shop, are third-generation citrus growers committed to selling the best-tasting citrus and reviving heirloom varieties like the Page orange.

If you can't find Pages, that's okay. Substitute any kind of mandarin you can lay your hands on, including satsumas or clementines. Zest the navels (or Valencias), rather than the Pages or tangerines. This syrup is featured in the Orangenius float (page 96) and the Orange Egg Cream (page 107).

½ cup (4 ounces) water

1 cup plus 2 tablespoons (9 ounces) cane sugar

1½ teaspoons freshly grated orange zest

¼ cup (2 ounces) freshly squeezed orange juice

¾ cup (6 ounces) freshly squeezed tangerine juice

Put the ½ cup water in a saucepan and pour the sugar into the water. Bring to a boil over medium heat, stirring gently from time to time to release any sugar that may be stuck to the bottom of the pan. Cook until the sugar has dissolved, about 10 minutes. Remove from the heat and add the orange zest. Let the syrup cool to room temperature. Add the orange and tangerine juices and stir. Chill before using.

Store the syrup in covered glass jars or plastic containers in the refrigerator for up to 2 weeks. The syrup may also be frozen in plastic containers for up to 3 months. If frozen, allow to thaw in the refrigerator overnight before using.

To make an orange soda, fill a 12-ounce glass halfway with ice, add ¼ cup (2 ounces) of Orange Syrup, top with seltzer, and stir gently with a soda spoon to combine. To make orangeade, follow the directions for making an orange soda, substituting flat water for the seltzer.

PINEAPPLE SYRUP

Because pineapple season arrives in the depths of winter in the Northeast, it makes us very happy. To pick a pineapple, look for one that is sporting some patches of yellow and gives slightly when you press on it with your thumb. The true test, however, is to sniff at the end of the pineapple where it was cut off the stalk. Does it smell the yummy way a pineapple ought to smell? If the answer is yes, then it's ready.

Be sure to start this recipe the day before you want to serve it, since the pineapple needs to marinate overnight. This syrup is featured in the the Lo-Co-Co float (page 93).

2 cups (16 ounces) cane sugar

1 cup (8 ounces) water

1 ripe medium pineapple, peeled, cored, and cut in ½-inch cubes

1 teaspoon freshly squeezed lemon juice

Combine the sugar and the 1 cup water in a large bowl. Stir the pineapple and lemon juice into the sugar-water mixture. Cover with plastic wrap and refrigerate for 24 hours, stirring occasionally, until the sugar has dissolved. If at the end of 24 hours there is still residual sugar at the bottom of the bowl, use a rubber spatula to loosen it and then stir vigorously until the sugar dissolves.

Strain the mixture over a bowl. The liquid in the bowl is your Pineapple Syrup. What's left in the strainer is Marinated Pineapple (page 171), which can be used as an ice cream topping or in the Flyin' Hawaiian Sundae (page 122). Voilà, you just made two recipes in one!

Chill the syrup before using it. Store the syrup in covered glass jars or plastic containers in the refrigerator for up to 2 weeks. The syrup may also be frozen in plastic containers for up to 3 months. The Marinated Pineapple can be stored in the same manner. If frozen, allow to thaw in the refrigerator overnight before using.

To make a pineapple soda, fill a 12-ounce glass halfway with ice, add ¼ cup (2 ounces) of Pineapple Syrup, top with seltzer, and stir gently with a soda spoon to combine.

RASPBERRY SYRUP

MAKES 4 CUPS

You don't have to wait for raspberry season to make this syrup. Frozen raspberries are easy to find and make as tasty a syrup as fresh raspberries do. The resulting syrup is a ruby-hued beauty that mixes well with lots of other syrup flavors. Try it in combination with lemon, lime, or pineapple. This syrup is featured in the Princess float (page 90).

2 pints fresh raspberries, or 24 ounces frozen raspberries

2 cups (16 ounces) cane sugar, or more depending on the tartness of the berries

5 teaspoons freshly squeezed lemon juice

1¼ cups (10 ounces) water

1 tablespoon honey

Put the raspberries and sugar in a saucepan. Stir briskly, mashing a few raspberries in the process. Cover and let sit at room temperature for 30 minutes. Add the lemon juice and water and bring to a boil over medium heat, stirring occasionally. Decrease the heat and simmer, uncovered, for 5 minutes. Remove from the heat and stir in the honey.

Place a fine-mesh strainer over a bowl and pour the berry mixture into it in manageable batches, using a wooden spoon to mash the mixture against the mesh of the strainer. Discard the seedy mash that remains in the strainer. Let the syrup cool to room temperature and chill before using.

Store the syrup in covered glass jars or plastic containers in the refrigerator for up to 2 weeks. The syrup may also be frozen in plastic containers for up to 3 months. If frozen, allow to thaw in the refrigerator overnight before using.

To make a raspberry soda, fill a 12-ounce glass halfway with ice, add ¼ cup (2 ounces) of Raspberry Syrup, top with seltzer, and stir gently with a soda spoon to combine.

STRAWBERRY SYRUP

Strawberries occupy a special place in our hearts because they herald the arrival of summer. We do a little dance when we first see them at the farmers' market because it means long days full of sunshine have finally arrived. Strawberry season usually begins sometime around Father's Day in the Northeast. If purchasing your strawberries at a farmers' market, seek out the most tender and perfectly ripe strawberries you can. They will give up more juice than their supermarket counterparts. Frozen strawberries may be used if fresh ones are not an option. This syrup is featured in the Strawberry Fields float (page 90).

4 quarts fresh strawberries, or 5 pounds frozen strawberries

1¾ cups plus 2 tablespoons (15 ounces) cane sugar, or more depending on the tartness of the berries

2 teaspoons freshly squeezed lemon juice

Wash and hull the strawberries, discarding any that are bad and cutting away soft spots as necessary. Halve or quarter larger berries so that all berries are in pieces no bigger than 1 inch. Set aside one-fourth of the berries. Place the remaining berries and sugar in a large saucepan, stir, cover, and let sit at room temperature for 15 minutes (this will draw the juice out of the berries). Bring the berries to a boil over medium heat. Decrease the heat and simmer, uncovered, for 5 minutes. Remove from the heat and using a potato (or bean) masher, mash the mixture in the saucepan 15 times. Add the remaining berries and lemon juice. Allow to cool for 15 minutes before proceeding to the next step.

Place a strainer over a bowl and pour the berry mixture into it in manageable batches, stirring to release the liquid. The liquid in the bowl is your Strawberry Syrup. What's left in the strainer is Strawberry Compote (page 168), which can be used as an ice cream topping or in the Berry Shortcake Crumble sundae (page 134). Voilà, you just made two recipes in one! Store the syrup in covered glass jars or plastic containers in the refrigerator for up to 2 weeks. The syrup may also be frozen in plastic containers for up to 3 months. The compote can be stored in the same manner. If frozen, allow to thaw in the refrigerator overnight before using.

To make a strawberry soda, fill a 12-ounce glass halfway with ice, add ¼ cup (2 ounces) of Strawberry Syrup, top with seltzer, and stir gently with a soda spoon to combine.

CONCORD GRAPE SYRUP

The story of the Concord grape is as distinctly American as the story of the soda fountain.

Developed in 1849 by Ephraim Wales Bull in Concord, Massachusetts, the grape took first place at the 1853 Boston Horticultural Society Exhibition and made its debut in the marketplace in 1854. Dr. Thomas Bramwell Welch, an ardent follower of the temperance movement, saw in the grape the possibility for creating a nonalcoholic sacramental wine. He began to market Dr. Welch's Unfermented Wine in 1869, but it was his son, Charles Edgar Welch, who would eventually propel the Concord grape to prominence. He doggedly marketed his father's grape juice, finally receiving a boost when he operated a concession at the 1893 Chicago World's Fair. Welch incorporated the Welch Grape Juice Company on April 19, 1897 and completed construction of a production facility in Westfield, New York, capable of producing 350,000 gallons of grape juice per year. Welch's factory building is now listed on the National Register of Historic Places. Westfield, New York, is known as the "Grape Juice Capital of the World," sitting plunk in the middle of the Lake Erie Concord Grape Belt, which was designated a New York State Heritage Area in 2006—the first recognized state agricultural heritage area in the United States.

A search through *The Dispenser's Formulary*, a book of recipes compiled by the editors of *The Soda Fountain* magazine in 1925, reveals a plethora of Concord grape–based recipes, from ice cream to hot grapeade to grape shakes that incorporate a raw egg. Our homage to the Concord grape comes in the form of a really grape-y syrup that can be used to make sparkling grape soda (opposite) or The Purple Cow float (page 94).

Purple Cow
I never saw a Purple Cow,
I never hope to see one;
But I can tell you, anyhow,
I'd rather see than be one.
—Gelett Burgess

CONCORD GRAPE SYRUP

Concord grapes are an early fall crop that show up in New York farmers' markets in the latter half of September. Although they were developed for the New England climate, they're grown all over the United States (although mostly in the northern states). Unless yours is a very large or sophisticated grocery store, you will probably not find Concord grapes on its shelves. Farmers' markets are your best bet, followed by health food stores that carry a good selection of produce.

Chances are you don't have a bottle of orange flower water hanging around in your pantry as it's not a commonly used ingredient in this country. If you need to locate some, try a store that has a well-curated herb and spice section. If you can wait for it to be shipped, it can be found easily enough online. (What to do with the rest of bottle once you've made grape syrup? Splash it in your bath. No kidding. It smells heavenly.) This syrup is featured in the Purple Cow float (page 94).

3½ pounds fresh Concord grapes, stemmed

1¾ cups (14 ounces) cane sugar

⅔ cup (5.4 ounces) water

5 teaspoons freshly squeezed lime juice

¼ teaspoon orange flower water (optional)

Place the grapes, sugar, the ⅔ cup water, and lime juice in a saucepan. Bring to a boil over medium heat. Decrease the heat and simmer, uncovered, for 10 minutes, stirring occasionally. Remove from the heat, let cool for 10 minutes, and stir in the orange flower water.

Place a strainer over a bowl and pour the grape mixture into it in manageable batches, using a wooden spoon to mash the mixture against the mesh of the strainer. Discard the seedy mash that remains in the strainer. Let the syrup cool to room temperature and chill before using.

Store the syrup in covered glass jars or plastic containers in the refrigerator for up to 2 weeks, but watch it, grapes do ferment! The syrup may also be frozen in plastic containers for up to 3 months. If frozen, allow to thaw in the refrigerator overnight before using.

To make a Concord grape soda, fill a 12-ounce glass halfway with ice, add ¼ cup (2 ounces) of Concord Grape Syrup, top with seltzer, and stir gently with a soda spoon to combine.

NOT IN A TEMPERANCE MOOD?

Farmacy's syrups are delightful in sodas and, not surprisingly, enchanting in cocktails. After we opened, it didn't take long before local watering holes started asking to experiment with our syrups. These are some of our favorites!

CHERRY OH BABY
MAKES 1 COCKTAIL

1.5 ounces white rum
0.5 ounce Cherry Heering liqueur
0.5 ounce freshly squeezed lime juice
0.75 ounce Cola Syrup (page 64)
Seltzer

Method: Build all ingredients in a Collins glass with ice, add seltzer to fill, and stir with a bar spoon.

Garnish: Lime wheel skewered with maraschino cherry

COLA SOUR
MAKES 1 COCKTAIL

2 ounces bourbon or rye
1.5 ounces freshly squeezed lemon juice
0.75 ounce Cola Syrup (page 64)
Dash of egg white

Method: Dry shake all ingredients in a cocktail shaker. Add ice and shake again. Strain over a rocks glass with ice.

Garnish: Maraschino cherry or orange twist

NEWLY FASHIONED
MAKES 1 COCKTAIL

3 ounces bourbon or rye
0.5 ounce Cola Syrup (page 64)
3 dashes cherry bitters
Splash of seltzer

Method: Build in a rocks glass, add ice, and stir.

Garnish: Orange twist with maraschino cherry

LA BATANGA
MAKES 1 COCKTAIL

2 ounces blanco tequila
0.5 ounce freshly squeezed lime juice
0.75 ounce Cola Syrup (page 64)
Seltzer

Method: Build in a pint glass with ice, top with seltzer to fill, and stir.

Garnish: Lime wedge

BASIL GIMLET
MAKES 1 COCKTAIL

2 ounces gin or vodka
1 ounce freshly squeezed lime juice
0.5 ounce Lime Syrup (page 71)
4 fresh basil leaves

Method: Place ingredients in a cocktail shaker and shake vigorously. Pour into a chilled martini glass.

Garnish: Lime wheel

LOVITO
MAKES 1 COCKTAIL

4 lovage leaves
3 lime wedges
0.75 ounce Lime Syrup (page 71)
2 ounces white rum
Seltzer

Method: Muddle lovage, lime, and syrup in cocktail shaker; add rum and shake vigorously. Pour into a Collins glass and fill with seltzer.

Garnish: Lovage leaf

Cocktails courtesy of Aaron Gretzinger and Colonie Restaurant, Brooklyn, NY

DARK & STORMY

MAKES 1 COCKTAIL

2 ounces dark rum
0.5 ounce freshly squeezed lime juice
0.75 ounce Ginger Syrup (page 66)
Dash of Angostura bitters
Seltzer

Method: Build ingredients in a Collins glass, stir with a bar spoon, and fill with seltzer.

Garnish: Lime wedge with candied ginger on skewer

THE BK ROCKET COCKTAIL

MAKES 1 COCKTAIL

2 ounces Cacao Prieto Don Rafael rum
0.5 ounce Faretti biscotti liqueur
0.5 ounce Coffee Syrup (page 62)

Method: Add all the ingredients to a cocktail shaker; shake and strain into a cordial glass.

Garnish: Shaved nutmeg

THE WIMBLEDON

MAKES 1 COCKTAIL

4 strawberries
2 ounces gin
0.25 ounce Strawberry Syrup (page 77)
0.25 ounce Lime Syrup (page 71)
1 ounce heavy cream

Method: Muddle the strawberries and syrup in a shaker; add the gin and cream. Shake vigorously and strain into a Collins glass filled with ice.

Garnish: Skewered strawberries

PERFECT PIMM'S

MAKES 1 COCKTAIL

2 ounces Pimm's
0.75 ounce Ginger Syrup (page 66)
Seltzer

Method: Build ingredients in a Collins glass, fill with seltzer, and stir with a bar spoon.

Garnish: Mint sprig, half-moon orange slice, and cucumber spear

PINEAPPLE PISCO SOUR

MAKES 1 COCKTAIL

2 ounces pisco
1 ounce freshly squeezed lemon juice
0.5 ounce Pineapple Syrup (page 75)
1 ounce fresh pineapple juice

Method: Dry shake ingredients in cocktail shaker, then shake again with ice. Pour into a rocks glass without ice.

Garnish: Three dashes Angostura bitters and crushed red peppercorns

PEACE CORPS

MAKES 1 COCKTAIL

1.5 ounces pisco
0.5 ounce Aperol
0.5 ounce Orange Syrup (page 74)
0.5 ounce freshly squeezed lemon juice
3 dashes orange bitters
Sparkling wine

Method: Shake pisco, Aperol, syrup, lemon juice, and bitters in a cocktail shaker and strain into wine glass with ice. Top with sparkling wine.

Garnish: Lemon wheel

NAWLINS TODDY

MAKES 1 COCKTAIL

2 ounces Sazerac rye
1 ounce New Orleans Mead Syrup (page 72)
Green tea

Method: Place ingredients in a heated mug and stir.

Garnish: Lime wheel with clove spoke

MEAD JULEP

MAKES 1 COCKTAIL

2 ounces bourbon
0.75 ounce New Orleans Mead Syrup (page 72)
4 sprigs fresh mint

Method: Place ingredients in a cocktail shaker and shake vigorously. Pour over crushed ice in a julep glass.

Garnish: Mint sprig

CHAPTER EIGHT

FLOATS

When you walk into our fountain, you're watching art in motion—preparing a float is a perfect opportunity to show off soda fountain craft and soda jerk flair. Fun to invent and a joy to name, an ice cream float is beautiful to behold.

"Sip it down a bit first!" we tell our customers. Because in the excitement of the moment, some people can't help but plunge that scoop of ice cream straight down into the soda. And that's a recipe for a sticky counter. (Which is okay, too.)

The first float was called an "ice cream soda." But, for the record, it didn't have any ice cream in it. That's right. Just ice, cream, and soda. Got it?

We have to thank Robert Green for the float that we know today. A soda vendor serving a busy crowd at an 1872 fair in Philadelphia, Green ran out of cream so he substituted ice cream, available from the concessionaire next door. The ice cream soda was born.

There are plenty of others who have claimed to have invented the ice cream soda: Fred Sanders in Detroit; Henry Bingle in Alexandria, Virginia; and Philip Mohr of Elizabeth, New Jersey among them. Another story comes from a New York City confectioner who allowed some of his regular customers—grimy newsboys—to experiment with the stock.

The fact is, given the prevalence of ice cream, soda, and creativity in the fountains of the last quarter of the nineteenth century, it's not hard to imagine that the idea of combining all three was happening all across America.

By 1934, *Ice Cream Trade* had declared the ice cream soda "a characteristically American product along with baseball, skyscrapers, hot biscuits . . . rough-riding cowboys and hooked rugs."

Take that, apple pie.

GENERAL METHOD

Making a float that tastes good isn't rocket science. Ice cream and soda, shucks, they kinda just go together. However, creating a float with a perfectly round scoop of ice cream perched just so on the side of the glass, well, we have to admit, takes a bit of practice. The technique for each of the Farmacy Floats is the same. Once you get the hang of it, you'll be chomping at the bit to host an ice cream float party to impress your guests. We can attest that some of the most picturesque celebrations

at Brooklyn Farmacy have included a round of brilliantly colored ice cream floats.

The following technique should be used when building any of the following Farmacy Floats with the exception of the Flatbush Ave. (page 98) and the Hot Flash (page 98).

To make an ice cream float, pour ¼ cup (2 ounces) of soda syrup (pages 59–79) into a fountain glass and add seltzer until the glass is two-thirds full. Stir gently with a fountain spoon to combine. Then, scoop a very firm 4-ounce ball of ice cream (about the size of a tennis ball) and "hang" the scoop on the inside rim of the glass. To hang the scoop of ice cream, stabilize the glass with one hand and utilize the scoop with your other hand to push the ball of ice cream down and out onto the rim of the glass so that the rim extends about two thirds of the way into the scoop. You don't want your scoop to feel like it could topple, but you also don't want to push down so hard that it splits. If you started with a firm scoop, you shouldn't need to make any adjustments to your ball of ice cream once it's hanging on the rim. Add the remaining seltzer to fill the glass. Drizzle a little bit of soda syrup onto the scoop of ice cream for decoration. Place the glass on a small plate and serve with a soda spoon and a soda straw.

TOOLS

4-ounce ice cream scoop

12-ounce fountain glass

Soda spoon

Soda straw

Dessert plate

BETTY BOOP

An old time favorite, some folks call this the black-and-white of floats. You can switch it up by reversing the ingredients and using vanilla syrup and chocolate ice cream. Either way, it's a "boop-oop-a-doop" of a float.

¼ cup (2 ounces) Fox's U-Bet chocolate syrup

1¼ cups (10 ounces) plain cold seltzer

1 (4-ounce) scoop vanilla ice cream

Pour the syrup into a fountain glass and add seltzer until the glass is two-thirds full. Stir gently with a soda spoon to combine. Then, scoop a very firm 4-ounce ball of ice cream and "hang" it on the inside rim of the glass. Add the remaining seltzer to fill the glass. Serve immediately.

HEY, PUMPKIN!

When the leaves begin to fall, this seasonal float says it all.

¼ cup (2 ounces) Ginger
Syrup (page 66)

1¼ cups (10 ounces) plain
cold seltzer

1 (4-ounce) scoop pumpkin
ice cream

Pour the syrup into a fountain glass and add seltzer until the glass is two-thirds full. Stir gently with a soda spoon to combine. Then, scoop a very firm 4-ounce ball of ice cream and "hang" it on the inside rim of the glass. Add the remaining seltzer to fill the glass. Serve immediately.

CHOCO-COLA

Two great flavors make for a dark and delicious float. The spice in the Cola Syrup brings out the sweetness of the chocolate ice cream. This is one of our most popular floats.

¼ cup (2 ounces) Cola Syrup
(page 64)

1¼ cups (10 ounces) plain
cold seltzer

1 (4-ounce) scoop chocolate
ice cream

Pour the syrup into a fountain glass and add seltzer until the glass is two-thirds full. Stir gently with a soda spoon to combine. Then, scoop a very firm 4-ounce ball of ice cream and "hang" it on the inside rim of the glass. Add the remaining seltzer to fill the glass. Serve immediately.

THE DALMATIAN

This float would have Cruella De Vil asking for one hundred more. This float is as cute as a puppy, and tasty to boot.

¼ cup (2 ounces) Lemon Syrup (page 71)

1¼ cups (10 ounces) plain cold seltzer

1 (4-ounce) scoop mint chocolate chip ice cream

Pour the syrup into a fountain glass and add seltzer until the glass is two-thirds full. Stir gently with a soda spoon to combine. Then, scoop a very firm 4-ounce ball of ice cream and "hang" it on the inside rim of the glass. Add the remaining seltzer to fill the glass. Serve immediately.

TARTY PANTS

MAKES 1 FLOAT

Sweet and tart, we named this float for the smart kids in the 'hood. (You know who you are!)

¼ cup (2 ounces) Lime Syrup (page 71)

1¼ cups (10 ounces) plain cold seltzer

1 (4-ounce) scoop vanilla ice cream

Pour the syrup into a fountain glass and add seltzer until the glass is two-thirds full. Stir gently with a soda spoon to combine. Then, scoop a very firm 4-ounce ball of ice cream and "hang" it on the inside rim of the glass. Add the remaining seltzer to fill the glass. Serve immediately.

THE TOOTSIE

Named after our favorite lolly, this float has quickly become beloved by kids, and funnily enough, grandpas!

¼ cup (2 ounces) Cherry Syrup
(page 60)

1¼ cups (10 ounces) plain
cold seltzer

1 (4-ounce) scoop chocolate
ice cream

Pour the syrup into a fountain glass and add seltzer until the glass is two-thirds full. Stir gently with a soda spoon to combine. Then, scoop a very firm 4-ounce ball of ice cream and "hang" it on the inside rim of the glass. Add the remaining seltzer to fill the glass. Serve immediately.

THE VIOLET

Named for our smartest soda jerk. She's pretty too. (The float is pictured at left.)

¼ cup (2 ounces) Fox's U-Bet
vanilla syrup

1¼ cups (10 ounces) plain
cold seltzer

1 (4-ounce) scoop black
raspberry ice cream

Pour the syrup into a fountain glass and add seltzer until the glass is two-thirds full. Stir gently with a soda spoon to combine. Then, scoop a very firm 4-ounce ball of ice cream and "hang" it on the inside rim of the glass. Add the remaining seltzer to fill the glass. Serve immediately.

PRINCESS FLOAT

If you know someone who loves the color pink, this float delivers!

¼ cup (2 ounces) Raspberry
Syrup (page 76)

1¼ cups (10 ounces) plain
cold seltzer

1 (4-ounce) scoop vanilla
ice cream

Pour the syrup into a fountain glass and add seltzer until the glass is
two-thirds full. Stir gently with a soda spoon to combine. Then, scoop a
very firm 4-ounce ball of ice cream and "hang" it on the inside rim of the
glass. Add the remaining seltzer to fill the glass. Serve immediately.

STRAWBERRY FIELDS

A perfect way to celebrate the start of summer, this very berry float is also charming to behold.

¼ cup (2 ounces) Strawberry
Syrup (page 77)

1¼ cups (10 ounces) plain
cold seltzer

1 (4-ounce) scoop strawberry
ice cream

Pour the syrup into a fountain glass and add seltzer until the glass is
two-thirds full. Stir gently with a soda spoon to combine. Then, scoop a
very firm 4-ounce ball of ice cream and "hang" it on the inside rim of the
glass. Add the remaining seltzer to fill the glass. Serve immediately.

THE JOEY

This float combination is super smooth, just like its namesake.

¼ cup (2 ounces) Vanilla Cream Syrup (page 59)

1¼ cups (10 ounces) plain cold seltzer

1 (4-ounce) scoop vanilla ice cream

Pour the syrup into a fountain glass and add seltzer until the glass is two-thirds full. Stir gently with a soda spoon to combine. Then, scoop a very firm 4-ounce ball of ice cream and "hang" it on the inside rim of the glass. Add the remaining seltzer to fill the glass. Serve immediately.

PURPLE HAZE

Both a nod to Jimi, and a reference to the heat wave we were enduring when we created this delicious summertime float.

¼ cup (2 ounces) Blueberry Syrup (page 65)

1¼ cups (10 ounces) plain cold seltzer

1 (4-ounce) scoop vanilla ice cream

Pour the syrup into a fountain glass and add seltzer until the glass is two-thirds full. Stir gently with a soda spoon to combine. Then, scoop a very firm 4-ounce ball of ice cream and "hang" it on the inside rim of the glass. Add the remaining seltzer to fill the glass. Serve immediately.

RHAPSODY IN BLUE

We're pretty sure Gershwin would enjoy this float.

¼ cup (2 ounces) Blueberry
Syrup (page 65)

1¼ cups (10 ounces) plain
cold seltzer

1 (4-ounce) scoop black
raspberry ice cream

Pour the syrup into a fountain glass and add seltzer until the glass is
two-thirds full. Stir gently with a soda spoon to combine. Then, scoop a
very firm 4-ounce ball of ice cream and "hang" it on the inside rim of the
glass. Add the remaining seltzer to fill the glass. Serve immediately.

THE KIKI

Spicy and sweet and named after one of our regulars, because yes, she's all that. Fountain purists may
argue that this float is called a "Boston Cooler."

¼ cup (2 ounces) Ginger Syrup
(page 66)

1¼ cups (10 ounces) plain
cold seltzer

1 (4-ounce) scoop vanilla
ice cream

Pour the soda syrup into a fountain glass and add seltzer until the
glass is two-thirds full. Stir gently with a fountain spoon to combine.
Then, scoop a very firm 4-ounce ball of ice cream and "hang" it on
the inside rim of the glass. Add the remaining seltzer to fill the glass.
Serve immediately.

THE LO-CO-CO

We all go a little crazy in the Northeast come February. This tropical float transports us to warm sandy beaches.

¼ cup (2 ounces) Pineapple Syrup (page 75)

1¼ cups (10 ounces) plain cold seltzer

1 (4-ounce) scoop coconut ice cream

Pour the syrup into a fountain glass and add seltzer until the glass is two-thirds full. Stir gently with a soda spoon to combine. Then, scoop a very firm 4-ounce ball of ice cream and "hang" it on the inside rim of the glass. Add the remaining seltzer to fill the glass. Serve immediately.

THE WAKE-UP CALL

MAKES 1 FLOAT

This one delivers a punch just when you need it.

¼ cup (2 ounces) Coffee Syrup (page 62)

1¼ cups (10 ounces) plain cold seltzer

1 (4-ounce) scoop coffee ice cream

Pour the syrup into a fountain glass and add seltzer until the glass is two-thirds full. Stir gently with a soda spoon to combine. Then, scoop a very firm 4-ounce ball of ice cream and "hang" it on the inside rim of the glass. Add the remaining seltzer to fill the glass. Serve immediately.

THE SANTA

Skip the plate of cookies—this is what he really wants! For a special presentation, add a red-and-white striped candy cane alongside the straw.

¼ cup (2 ounces) Fox's U-Bet chocolate syrup

1¼ cups (10 ounces) plain cold seltzer

1 (4-ounce) scoop peppermint stick ice cream

Pour the syrup into a fountain glass and add seltzer until the glass is two-thirds full. Stir gently with a soda spoon to combine. Then, scoop a very firm 4-ounce ball of ice cream and "hang" it on the inside rim of the glass. Add the remaining seltzer to fill the glass. Serve immediately.

PURPLE COW

First there was an ode (see page 78), then came the float, pictured at right.

¼ cup (2 ounces) Concord Grape Syrup (page 79)

1¼ cups (10 ounces) plain cold seltzer

1 (4-ounce) scoop vanilla ice cream

Pour the syrup into a fountain glass and add seltzer until the glass is two-thirds full. Stir gently with a soda spoon to combine. Then, scoop a very firm 4-ounce ball of ice cream and "hang" it on the inside rim of the glass. Add the remaining seltzer to fill the glass. Serve immediately.

ORANGENIUS

Our mom's favorite ice cream bar, the Creamsicle, inspired us to create this lovely float.

¼ cup (2 ounces) Orange Syrup (page 74)

1¼ cups (10 ounces) plain cold seltzer

1 (4-ounce) scoop vanilla ice cream

Pour the syrup into a fountain glass and add seltzer until the glass is two-thirds full. Stir gently with a soda spoon to combine. Then, scoop a very firm 4-ounce ball of ice cream and "hang" it on the inside rim of the glass. Add the remaining seltzer to fill the glass. Serve immediately.

LET'S HEAD SOUTH

We hoped to create a little bit o' sunshine in winter with this float, and it does just that.

¼ cup (2 ounces) Pink Grapefruit Syrup (page 68)

1¼ cups (10 ounces) plain cold seltzer

1 (4-ounce) scoop vanilla ice cream

Pour the syrup into a fountain glass and add seltzer until the glass is two-thirds full. Stir gently with a soda spoon to combine. Then, scoop a very firm 4-ounce ball of ice cream and "hang" it on the inside rim of the glass. Add the remaining seltzer to fill the glass. Serve immediately.

THE PINK POODLE

The name for this float was inspired by the frothy pink tuft that appears when the hibiscus soda and vanilla ice cream meet.

¼ cup (2 ounces) Hibiscus Syrup (page 69)

1¼ cups (10 ounces) plain cold seltzer

1 (4-ounce) scoop vanilla ice cream

Pour the syrup into a fountain glass and add seltzer until the glass is two-thirds full. Stir gently with a soda spoon to combine. Then, scoop a very firm 4-ounce ball of ice cream and "hang" it on the inside rim of the glass. Add the remaining seltzer to fill the glass. Serve immediately.

GOSH NOG IT!

A great seasonal float that combines two holiday flavors perfectly.

¼ cup (2 ounces) New Orleans Mead Syrup (page 72)

1¼ cups (10 ounces) plain cold seltzer

1 (4-ounce) scoop eggnog ice cream

Pour the syrup into a fountain glass and add seltzer until the glass is two-thirds full. Stir gently with a soda spoon to combine. Then, scoop a very firm 4-ounce ball of ice cream and "hang" it on the inside rim of the glass. Add the remaining seltzer to fill the glass. Serve immediately.

HOT FLASH

It's hot? It's cold? True story: The first customers to order this float were three teenage boys. ("I'll have a Hot Flash." "Yeah, me too!" "Yeah, make it three Hot Flashes.") They didn't get the joke and it sure was hard to keep a straight face while taking that order! (Pictured at right.)

1½ cups (12 ounces) coffee or hot chocolate

1 (4-ounce) scoop vanilla, chocolate, or coffee ice cream

Pour the coffee or hot chocolate into a fountain glass until the glass is two-thirds full. Then, scoop a very firm 4-ounce ball of ice cream and "hang" the scoop on the inside rim of the glass. Add the remaining malted milk, coffee, or hot chocolate to fill the glass. Serve immediately.

FLATBUSH AVE.

This float combines two of our favorite things: egg creams and ice cream. Refer to the next chapter (page 101) for a full description of egg creams and how to make them.

¼ cup plus 2 tablespoons (3 ounces) cold whole milk

¾ cup (6 ounces) plain cold seltzer

3 tablespoons (1½ ounces) Fox's U-Bet chocolate or vanilla syrup

1 (4-ounce) scoop chocolate or vanilla ice cream

Pour the milk into a fountain glass and add seltzer until the glass is two-thirds full. Pour the syrup into the center of the glass and then gently push the back of a soda spoon into the center of the drink. Rock the spoon back and forth, keeping most of the action at the bottom of the glass, to incorporate the syrup without wrecking the froth.

Then, scoop a very firm 4-ounce ball of ice cream and "hang" it on the inside rim of the glass. Add the remaining seltzer to fill the glass. Serve immediately.

CHAPTER NINE

EGG CREAMS

For all its mystique, all you need to make an egg cream are three simple ingredients: milk, seltzer, and syrup. The devil (and the debate) is in the details—the order in which you add those ingredients and the nuances of technique. What you are aiming for is an ice-cold drink that leaves you with a white foam mustache when you slug it down without a straw.

Like the ice cream soda, the egg cream is a success that has many fathers. There are as many claimants to the title of "inventor of the egg cream" as there are techniques for making one. Maybe it was the widely-credited confectioner Louis Auster. Maybe it was your Uncle Hymie. But we're pretty sure that whoever it was, he was a New Yorker.

Here's our theory: the egg cream was born on the Lower East Side of Manhattan, a crowded immigrant community and the heart of Jewish America at the turn of the twentieth century. Then, as now, milk was delivered to the area along one route: from the Hudson Valley south through the Bronx, upper Manhattan, and Queens, and finally, down to the Lower East Side. In other words, the tenement families were the last to get their milk. Not at its freshest. But what was fresh, even in the urban slums, were eggs. There might not have been any cows on Delancey Street, but there were chickens on every rooftop east of Broadway.

So if you were a fountain operator on the Lower East Side and you wanted to serve your clientele a "fancy" drink for which you could charge a bit more, you would probably skip the milk, as well as the cream, and instead add a whipped-up egg white to top off a no-frills chocolate soda. The "cream" was the crème de la chicken, not the crème de la cow.

Again, that's just our theory. We're sticking with it. Until the next guy walks in with a better one.

GENERAL METHOD

The following technique applies to all of our egg cream recipes. To make an egg cream, pour milk into an egg cream glass and add seltzer until the froth comes right up to the top of the glass without overflowing. Slowly and steadily pour the syrup into one location in the center of the seltzer mixture. Using the back of a spoon, gently push the spoon into the drink in the spot where you added the syrup until the spoon hits the bottom of the glass. Rock the spoon back and forth, keeping most of the action at the bottom of the glass to incorporate the syrup without wrecking your froth. The resulting drink should be mostly brown (if it's chocolate) with a frothy white head on top about an inch high.

:: **TIP** :: To make a nondairy and vegan variation on a traditional egg cream, substitute almond milk for cow's milk and follow the instructions for making a Maple Egg Cream (page 106). This lactose-free egg cream was born to satisfy the requests of our customers with milk sensitivities. Although you can experiment with other cow's milk replacements, we found that almond milk produced the most satisfying and frothy results.

TOOLS

12-ounce egg cream glass

Soda spoon

BROOKLYN EGG CREAM

This is the most traditional of the egg creams, and the one that incites the most heated debate, both on its origins and the methods to make it. It's a lightly sweetened, bubbly drink that you can enjoy anytime (and which has about as many calories as a slice of buttered toast).

¼ cup plus 2 tablespoons (3 ounces) cold whole milk

¾ cup (6 ounces) plain cold seltzer

3 tablespoons (1½ ounces) Fox's U-Bet chocolate syrup

Pour the milk into an egg cream glass and add seltzer until froth comes up to the top of the glass. Pour the syrup into the center of the glass and then gently push the back of a spoon into the center of the drink. Rock the spoon back and forth, keeping most of the action at the bottom of the glass, to incorporate the syrup without wrecking the froth. Serve immediately.

IN BROOKLYNESE

For those of you who speak Brooklynese, here are the same instructions from Bobby Egg Cream, a Farmacy regular.

"So ya take two fingers of milk and measure from the bottom of the glass, see? Then, you add one finger of Fox's, see? So it's, you know, two-to-one. Now ya gotta add the seltzer. Your seltzer's cold? It's gotta be cold. Let the seltzer flow over a bit. Not too much! Put ya spoon in the glass and stir it, like this. See kid, back and forth. But not too hard! You don't want to beat the crap out of the seltzer."

MANHATTAN EGG CREAM

MAKES 1 EGG CREAM

In New York City, the boroughs, like brothers, often compete with each other, jostling and throwing elbows for attention and recognition. While the Brooklyn Egg Cream is the original (fugeddaboutit), it wouldn't be complete without its Manhattan counterpart.

¼ cup plus 2 tablespoons (3 ounces) cold whole milk

¾ cup (6 ounces) plain cold seltzer

3 tablespoons (1½ ounces) Fox's U-bet vanilla syrup

Pour the milk into an egg cream glass and add seltzer until froth comes up to the top of the glass. Pour the syrup into the center of the glass and then gently push the back of a spoon into the center of the drink. Rock the spoon back and forth, keeping most of the action at the bottom of the glass, to incorporate the syrup without wrecking the froth. Serve immediately.

THE SYRUP OF CHOICE

While folks could easily spend the rest of eternity quibbling about how to make a "real" egg cream, what goes into one has never been up for debate: cold seltzer, milk, and Fox's U-Bet syrup. Yes, according to egg cream purists, you can only use Fox's and that's that.

Perhaps that's because the histories of the egg cream and that of H. Fox & Co., maker of U-Bet, run parallel to one another. Sometime around 1900, Herman Fox starting making fruit toppings and chocolate and fruit syrups in his Brooklyn basement, and the first egg creams made with Fox's syrups appeared in 1904.

In the 1920s, Herman became a wildcatter and set out for Texas to try his hand at oil drilling. Although

he returned to Brooklyn without having struck black gold, he did hit on something priceless in the process: a name for his syrups. Apparently, wildcatters were quite fond of the affirmative phrase "you bet," so Herman adopted the name U-Bet for his syrups.

H. Fox & Co. remains a Brooklyn institution and it still occupies the building Herman moved into in the 1930s. Herman's son Irving joined the business in the 1940s, followed by Irving's son David in the 1960s. The company is now run by David's son Kelly, the fourth generation of Foxes to run the business. Now that's a Brooklyn story!

MAPLE EGG CREAM

Having spent part of our childhood in the backwoods of Maine, maple syrup was our sugar. It seemed only natural to find a way to include this astounding gift from nature on our menu. At the Farmacy, we use maple syrup from Rockwall Maple Farm, made in Maine by our former elementary school teachers, the Hamiltons.

¼ cup plus 2 tablespoons (3 ounces) cold whole milk

¾ cup (6 ounces) cold plain seltzer

3 tablespoons (1½ ounces) pure maple syrup

Pour the milk into an egg cream glass and add seltzer until froth comes up to the top of the glass. Pour the syrup into the center of the glass and then gently push the back of a spoon into the center of the drink. Rock the spoon back and forth, keeping most of the action at the bottom of the glass, to incorporate the syrup without wrecking the froth. Serve immediately.

COFFEE EGG CREAM

We couldn't take ourselves seriously if we didn't add our own take on the traditional egg cream with the syrups we make in our own kitchen. A "real egg cream" uses Fox's U-Bet, a point we wouldn't dream of arguing. That said, the Coffee Egg Cream was our first break from tradition. And by gosh, it's good.

¼ cup (2 ounces) cold whole milk

¾ cup (6 ounces) plain cold seltzer

¼ cup (2 ounces) Coffee Syrup (page 62)

Pour the milk into an egg cream glass and add seltzer until froth comes up to the top of the glass. Pour the syrup into the center of the glass and then gently push the back of a spoon into the center of the drink. Rock the spoon back and forth, keeping most of the action at the bottom of the glass, to incorporate the syrup without wrecking the froth. Serve immediately.

BLUEBERRY EGG CREAM

Another successful departure from the traditional egg cream, the Blueberry Egg Cream is an eagerly anticipated summer treat at the Farmacy. Not only is it tasty, it is a spectacular shade of purple.

¼ cup plus 2 tablespoons (3 ounces) cold whole milk

¾ cup (6 ounces) plain cold seltzer

3 tablespoons (1½ ounces) Blueberry Syrup (page 65)

Pour the milk into an egg cream glass and add seltzer until froth comes up to the top of the glass. Pour the syrup into the center of the glass and then gently push the back of a spoon into the center of the drink. Rock the spoon back and forth, keeping most of the action at the bottom of the glass, to incorporate the syrup without wrecking the froth. Serve immediately.

ORANGE EGG CREAM

If you like the combination of orange and cream, this one's for you. We owe the invention of this egg cream to a Farmacy customer who came into the fountain one day and asked if we could make an orange egg cream with our syrup. We did. He drank it, and then he proceeded to drink three more. When he departed, the soda jerks made a few for themselves to confirm the goodness. Boom, it was on the next menu!

¼ cup plus 2 tablespoons (3 ounces) cold whole milk

¾ cup (6 ounces) plain cold seltzer

3 tablespoons (1½ ounces) Orange Syrup (page 74)

Pour the milk into an egg cream glass and add seltzer until froth comes up to the top of the glass. Pour the syrup into the center of the glass and then gently push the back of a spoon into the center of the drink. Rock the spoon back and forth, keeping most of the action at the bottom of the glass, to incorporate the syrup without wrecking the froth. Serve immediately

CHAPTER TEN

SUNDAES

Our menu is a smorgasbord of sweets and treats, but the ice cream sundae is our pièce de résistance. From crafting it to christening it, the sundae is where we lavish all our creativity. Give our guidelines a wide berth—it's hard to ruin ice cream and you can't burn a sundae. Experiment. Mix it up. And remember, the best sundae is a study in contrast: salty and sweet, hot and cold, crunchy and smooth. Every spoonful should have a taste of each.

Ice cream has a long history as a frozen treat. Roman emperors, Napoleon, and our own Founding Fathers included it on menus to impress foreign potentates and ambassadors. But their versions were probably quite different from the smooth blended confection we know today.

That creation took its form in the mid-1800s with hand-cranked machines and mass production. By the turn of the century, ice cream was a fountain staple thanks to the happy accident of the ice cream soda and the versatility of the ice cream sundae. Consumption in the United States spiked from five million gallons annually in 1901 to 101 million gallons in 1919!

By 1920, ice cream was king, reigning as the "universal palliative to Prohibition woes" and as a happy mate for the "bereaved pretzel" abandoned by outlawed beer. During the Great Depression, the government commissioned experts to determine the nutritional value. They concluded that "Ice cream makes every meal a banquet of health!"

If that weren't commendation enough, World War II generals rewarded exceptional valor with extra ice cream rations, and the Pentagon prioritized it as a crucial for troop morale. The Navy even built a million dollar floating ice cream parlor that traveled from base to base throughout the Pacific.

TOOLS

Ice cream scoops, 2-ounce and 4-ounce

Soda spoons

Beehive sundae bowls

Tulip sundae dishes

Banana split boats

Stainless steel sherbet bowls (for miniature sundaes)

Dessert plates

WHAT'S THAT CHERRY DOING UP THERE?

Looking delicious. It's as easy as that.

The maraschino cherry wasn't always the pretty little ice-cream topper it is today. For centuries, it was just a small, dark, sour fruit growing wild on the coasts of the Adriatic. Its Italian name was marasca, from the Latin word *amarus*, meaning bitter, but it looked more like an olive than the bright pink kiss on top of a sundae. The Dalmatian locals pickled the fruit in seawater to preserve it through the winter.

Eventually, the marasca spread from the palaces of Europe to the gourmands of America, usually conveyed in a cocktail glass and always steeped in liqueur and red coloring rather than seawater. The marasca had become a maraschino . . . and a delicacy.

There's no definitive story as to how the cherry jumped from the cocktail to the sundae. The conflation of bar and fountain as Prohibition neared certainly helped. But what was most important in making the cherry a necessary item at the fountain was the work of Ernest Wiegrand. An Oregonian, Wiegrand spent years perfecting a curing process that worked well for virtually any variety of sweet cherry cultivated in America and, importantly, contained no alcohol. His formula, introduced in 1925, turned the maraschino from an imported delicacy into a homegrown industry and immortalized the bright red cherry as the signature of ice cream indulgence.

It's a long process—a month of brining to make a perfect cherry. And to think that we treat each one with about as much ceremony as a fortune cookie! Such is the fate of a garnish that answers as much to tradition as to taste.

THE ANYDAY SUNDAE

Before we get to sundaes that incorporate everything from bacon to coconut, let's start with the classic ice cream sundae, or as we call it, the Anyday Sundae. While any flavor ice cream may be used, vanilla is the most classic. You can scatter some rainbow sprinkles on the whipped cream if you'd like (a favorite with the kids at the Farmacy).

¼ cup Hot Fudge (page 161) or Caramel Sauce (page 162)

1 (2-ounce) scoop ice cream, loosely packed

1 (4-ounce) scoop ice cream, firmly packed

½ cup Whipped Cream (page 177)

1 maraschino cherry

Pour 2 tablespoons of the Hot Fudge or Caramel Sauce into a tulip sundae dish, beginning close to the top rim and rotating the dish while pouring, so that the sauce coats the entire inside of the dish. Place the 2-ounce scoop of ice cream in the bottom of the dish and press it down with the back of the scoop ("veins" of sauce should pop out from the ice cream). Place the 4-ounce scoop of ice cream on top of the first scoop, leaving a ½-inch "moat" around it (to accommodate your remaining sauce). Cover the second scoop with the remaining sauce, leaving a "bald spot" in the center (so the whipped cream doesn't slide off). Top with Whipped Cream and, finally, the maraschino cherry. Serve immediately.

THE AFFUGAZI AFFOGATO

We purchased our espresso machine with dreams of hot espresso sundaes and crazy coffee drink combinations. Days of caffeine-fueled experimentation resulted in the invention of one of our favorite sundaes. A Vanilla Cake (page 196) nestled in a beehive bowl serves as the base for this coffee concoction: The role the espresso-soaked vanilla cake plays is akin to that of lady fingers in the iconic tiramisu. It's a visual delight to watch the cake soak up the coffee, so save the last step of pouring the coffee into the sundae until you bring this dessert to the table. While this sundae is mind-bending with espresso, we've specified regularly brewed coffee in the ingredients for those of you who may not have an espresso machine at home.

1 Vanilla Cake (page 196)

1 (4-ounce) scoop vanilla ice cream

1 (2-ounce) scoop vanilla ice cream

¼ cup Awesome Chocolate Shell (page 164)

½ cup Whipped Cream (page 177)

Shaved chocolate (optional)

¼ cup freshly brewed strong coffee, hot

Put the Vanilla Cake in the center of the beehive sundae bowl. Use the back of a soup spoon to flatten one side of the 4-ounce scoop of ice cream and center the scoop flat side down on the top of the cake. Place the second scoop of ice cream on top of the first scoop. Drizzle 2 tablespoons of Awesome Chocolate Shell over the ice cream, allowing it to cascade down the sides. Let the shell harden, about 30 seconds, before proceeding with the next steps. Top with Whipped Cream and dust with shaved chocolate. Pour the coffee into the "moat" around the base of the Vanilla Cake. Serve immediately.

THE ALMOND JOYFUL

Inspired by one of our favorite candy bars and made with our Coconut Almond Macaroon Crumble (page 155), we debuted the Almond Joyful halfway through a bitter cold January when everyone was dreaming about where the coconuts grow. It was an immediate hit. When creating this incredibly delicious sundae, we invite you to channel your inner Willie Wonka, keeping in mind the composition of the one and only Almond Joy candy bar.

¼ cup Hot Fudge (page 161)

½ cup Coconut Almond Macaroon Crumble (page 155)

2 (4-ounce) scoops coconut ice cream, loosely packed

¾ cup Whipped Cream (page 177)

Shaved chocolate (optional)

Pour 2 tablespoons of Hot Fudge into the bottom of a banana split boat. Spread ¼ cup of the Coconut Almond Macaroon Crumble on top of the fudge. Place the two scoops of ice cream side by side on top of the crumble. Spread the remaining crumble on top of the ice cream and pour the remaining fudge over all. Top with Whipped Cream and shaved chocolate. Serve immediately.

DORIS SEYMOUR

The flavors and tastes of certain foods are a portal to our emotional vault of past experiences and feelings, instantly transporting us back to a moment in time. Whether or not you were a scout, most of you have had the pleasure of sitting around a campfire experiencing a nip in the air, the crackle of wood logs burning and the sounds of a summer night. And of course, the s'more.

Because you can't build a campfire in your kitchen, this sundae was designed to evoke that sittin'-around-the-campfire feeling. Using our Nutty-Ella, a chocolate-roasted hazelnut butter, we were able to recreate the smoky s'more flavor in an ice cream sundae.

This sundae is an homage to a classy couple we used to know, Doris and Seymour. (Seymour. S'more. Get it?)

½ cup **Amazing Graham Crumble** (page 153)

1 (4-ounce) scoop **vanilla ice cream**

1 (4-ounce) scoop **chocolate ice cream**

¼ cup **Nutty-Ella** (page 173)

⅓ cup **Whipped Cream** (page 177)

Shaved chocolate

Spread ¼ cup of the Amazing Graham Crumble in a banana split boat. Place scoops of ice cream side by side on top of the crumble. Spoon the Nutty-Ella on top of the ice cream. Cover with the remaining crumble. Top with Whipped Cream and dust with shaved chocolate. Serve immediately.

BANDANA SPLIT

There is a place in the fountain for bacon bits, potato chips, and other trendy toppings. But the classic banana split is such a perfect blend of ingredients that we figured staying with the basics would honor its proud history. We did however take the liberty to rename it after one of our favorite Brooklyn girl bands, The Bandana Splits. They filmed a music video for their song "Sometimes" at the soda fountain, and we named a sundae after them. That's fair, right?

1 ripe medium banana, halved lengthwise, with the skin on

1 (2-ounce) scoop vanilla ice cream

1 (2-ounce) scoop chocolate ice cream

1 (2-ounce) scoop coffee ice cream

¼ cup Hot Fudge (page 161)

2 tablespoons Caramel Sauce (page 162)

¾ cup Whipped Cream (page 177)

1 tablespoon walnuts, finely chopped (optional)

1 maraschino cherry

Place two scoops of ice cream side by side in a (you got it) banana split boat. Place the third scoop centered on top of the other two to create a "pyramid." Affix half of the banana, skin-side out, to either side of the ice cream scoops parallel with the long sides of the boat. Press on them gently to get them to adhere and then delicately peel off the skins. Be sure to leave some room in the bottom of the dish to accommodate the sauces. Pour the sauces over the ice cream, pouring the fudge on one side and the caramel sauce on the other side, leaving a "bald spot" in the center for your Whipped Cream. Top evenly with Whipped Cream and sprinkle the walnuts on top. Top with the cherry. Serve immediately.

COOKIE MONSTER

When designing a sundae, you can research and scheme all you want. Or, you can just lay out a bunch of things that taste really good, and make a sundae. Such was the case with creation of the Cookie Monster sundae, which is built on the rock-solid foundation of the beloved chocolate chip cookie. If anybody dares call your creation simplistic, just do what we do: throw some Cookie Monster blue sprinkles at them. And when in doubt, look to Sesame Street for inspiration. Me like it.

Although we recommend chocolate chip cookies, the Cookie Monster himself was an equal opportunity cookie eater. So, feel free to use any cookie you have around. As long as you sing "'C' is for Cookie" while you do, everything will be okay.

2 (4-ounce) scoops mint chocolate chip ice cream

1 cup Chocolate Chip Cookie Crumble (page 154)

¼ cup Hot Fudge (page 161)

½ cup Whipped Cream (page 177)

2 tablespoons walnuts, finely chopped

Blue sprinkles

Place 1 scoop of the ice cream in the center of a beehive sundae bowl. Press the second scoop firmly down on top of the first scoop, creating a double stack. Spread the crumble evenly over and around the ice cream in the bottom of the bowl. Drizzle the fudge over the crumble. Top with Whipped Cream and then walnuts. Dust the Whipped Cream heavily with an even coat of blue sprinkles. Serve immediately.

SPICE CAKE SUNDAE

This festive sundae says yes to having your cake and eating it, too. Eggnog ice cream married with moist Spice Cake and Caramel Sauce is a perfect dessert to celebrate the holidays from Thanksgiving straight through to New Year's Eve. Warming the cake for five minutes in a 300°F oven renders this sundae irresistible.

1⁄12 of a Spice Bundt Cake
(page 197)

1 (4-ounce) scoop eggnog
ice cream

1⁄4 cup Caramel Sauce (page 162)

3⁄4 cup Whipped Cream
(page 177)

Dash of freshly grated nutmeg

Halve the piece of cake to form two smaller wedges and lay the two pieces in a "V" shape in the center of a beehive sundae bowl. Press the scoop of ice cream into the center of the cake "V." Pour the caramel over the ice cream, leaving a "bald spot" for the Whipped Cream. Top with Whipped Cream and dust with nutmeg. Serve immediately.

THE GREAT PUMPKIN

Like Linus van Pelt sitting patiently in the pumpkin patch, we wait for pumpkin ice cream to make an appearance each October. But unlike Linus, we are rewarded with the arrival of the Great Pumpkin (sundae), and we rest assured that all is right with humankind.

½ cup Wet Walnuts (page 176)

1 (2-ounce) scoop pumpkin ice cream

1 (4-ounce) scoop pumpkin ice cream

½ cup Whipped Cream (page 177)

Pinch of ground cinnamon

Spoon ¼ cup of the walnuts into the bottom of a tulip sundae dish. Place the 2-ounce scoop of ice cream in the dish and gently press it down with the back of the scoop. Place the 4-ounce scoop of ice cream on top of the first scoop, leaving a ½-inch "moat" around it (to accommodate your remaining walnuts). Cover the second scoop with the remaining walnuts, leaving a "bald spot" in the center (so the Whipped Cream doesn't slide off). Top with the Whipped Cream and dust with cinnamon. Serve immediately.

FLYIN' HAWAIIAN

In the 1970s, the tiny Hawaiian island of Lanai produced 75 percent of the world's pineapples, and became affectionately known as "The Pineapple Isle." The pineapple plantation style of life has moved on, replaced by eco-tourism and retirees. Pineapples, of course, were a staple of the diet, but very rarely eaten without a sprinkling of powdered salty dried plum—*li hing mui* (Chinese for "traveling plum"). Brought to Hawaii by Chinese, *li hing mui* has a strong and distinctive flavor that boasts a unique combination of sweet, sour, and salty. By combining *li hing mui*, macadamia nuts, and coconut ice cream, we have formed not only a perfect sundae, but a perfect Hawaiian *hui* (meaning partnership).

Li hing mui powder may be found in Asian markets or online. It's also a welcome addition to mixed drinks and cocktails, especially those with a tequila base.

2 (4-ounce) scoops coconut ice cream

¾ cup Marinated Pineapple (page 171)

¼ cup Pineapple Syrup (page 75)

1 teaspoon *li hing mui* powder

¼ cup unsalted macadamia nuts, coarsely chopped

½ cup Whipped Cream (optional, page 177)

Place 1 scoop of the ice cream in the center of a beehive sundae bowl. Press the second scoop firmly down on top of the first scoop, creating a double stack. Spread the Marinated Pineapple evenly over and around the ice cream in the bottom of the bowl. Drizzle the Pineapple Syrup over the Marinated Pineapple. Sprinkle the *li hing mui* powder over the pineapple and then scatter the macadamia nuts over all. Top with Whipped Cream. Serve immediately.

HEY, BLONDIE!

MAKES 1 SUNDAE

While we discourage you from hollering this out while walking down the street, you're welcome to do so at our fountain. At its foundation, this salty sweet sundae features a beloved childhood treat.

1 Blondie square (page 181)

2 (4-ounce) scoops toffee ice cream

¼ cup Caramel Sauce (page 161)

½ cup Whipped Cream (page 177)

2 tablespoons roasted salted almonds, finely chopped

Place the Blondie in a beehive bowl, off to one side with a corner pointing down into the center of the bowl. Place the two scoops of ice cream side by side with the Blondie poking up from between them. Drizzle the sauce on the Blondie and around the sides of the ice cream, leaving a "bald spot" for the Whipped Cream. Top with Whipped Cream and scatter the almonds over the Whipped Cream. Serve immediately.

SIMI'S SUNDAE

MAKES 1 SUNDAE

Named for the wife of our ice cream maker at Adirondack Creamery, whose recipe for pistachio cardamom kulfi (a dense frozen Indian dessert) was the inspiration for Adirondack Creamery's pistachio cardamom ice cream.

⅓ cup Pistachio Crumble (page 158)

1 (2-ounce) scoop pistachio ice cream

1 (4-ounce) scoop pistachio ice cream

¼ cup Caramel Sauce (page 161)

¼ cup Whipped Cream (page 177)

Spoon ¼ cup of the crumble into the bottom of a tulip sundae dish. Place the 2-ounce scoop of ice cream in the dish and gently press it down with the back of the scoop. Place the 4-ounce scoop of ice cream on top of the first scoop, leaving a ½-inch "moat" around it (to accommodate your sauce and remaining crumble). Pour the sauce over the ice cream and cover with the remaining crumble. Top with Whipped Cream. Serve immediately.

HOT MAMA

This spicy sundae debuted on Mother's Day 2012, and features our Hot Mama Crumble. The flavor of the crumble is reminiscent of Mexican hot chocolate. The coffee ice cream was selected because, as we all know, moms need caffeine as much as they need chocolate.

¼ cup Hot Fudge (page 161)

½ cup Hot Mama Crumble
(page 156)

2 (4-ounce) scoops coffee
ice cream, loosely packed

¾ cup Whipped Cream
(page 177)

Shaved chocolate

1 maraschino cherry

Pour 2 tablespoons of fudge into the bottom of a banana split boat. Spread ¼ cup of the crumble on top of the fudge. Place the two scoops of ice cream side by side on top of the crumble. Spread the remaining crumble on top of the ice cream and pour the remaining fudge over all. Top with Whipped Cream, shaved chocolate, and a maraschino cherry. Serve immediately.

HOG ON A HOT TIN ROOF

The wooden shelves at the Farmacy are lined with locally made products like preserves, sauces, and goodness-to-go like the Redhead's Bacon Peanut Brittles. With their tag line, "Everything is better with bacon" (we agree), these roasted peanuts feature maple syrup, cayenne, and yes, bacon. All it took for us was to pop open a bag and from there, it was a quick leap to making this handsome sundae (pictured opposite). See Resources (page 206) for ordering the Redhead's Bacon Peanut Brittles.

2 (4-ounce) scoops vanilla
ice cream

¼ cup Hot Fudge (page 161)

¼ cup The Redhead's Bacon
Peanut Brittles

½ cup Whipped Cream (page 177)

Place the two scoops of ice cream side by side in the bottom of a banana split boat and cover with fudge. Scatter the brittles over the fudge and top each scoop individually with ¼ cup of Whipped Cream. Serve immediately.

MAKIN' WHOOPIE! SUNDAE

This sundae is a tribute to the late Eddie Cantor's famous song and is dedicated to all the loving couples who enter our retro time machine for an old-fashioned romantic escape. On a Friday night at our soda fountain, the lights are dimmed, Ella Fitzgerald croons over the speakers, and sweet treats are made for two. The Makin' Whoopie Sundae, with sweet ice cream nestled between chocolate cake buns, has the potential to be a real baby-maker.

We've also noticed that this sundae is a favorite among red-faced adolescents, who strain to hold back uncontrollable giggles as they take turns ordering the "Makin' Whoopie." So, for the romantic in you who wants to take a trip down memory lane, or for the kid in all of us who simply wants to say something that hangs on the edge of the inappropriate, this sundae is for you.

2 Chocolate Whoopie Cakes (page 188)

1 (4-ounce) scoop chocolate ice cream

1 (4-ounce) scoop vanilla ice cream

¼ cup Hot Fudge (page 161)

½ cup Whipped Cream (page 177)

Shaved chocolate

2 maraschino cherries

Place the two scoops of ice cream side by side in the bottom of a banana split boat. Pour the fudge over the ice cream, leaving a "bald spot" for your Whipped Cream. Place the cakes on opposite sides of the boat with the flat sides of the cakes facing each other and press gently to affix them to the scoops of ice cream. Top with whipped cream and shaved chocolate. Finally, top with the two maraschino cherries, stems intertwined. Serve immediately.

THE BROWNIE SUNDAE

In a world of sundaes that push the boundaries of unique sweets to the edge, the straightforward Brownie Sundae never fails to deliver. It is, hands down, one of the most popular sundaes at the Farmacy. If you are looking for something that can have your guests, young and old, singing your name in praise, make a Brownie Sundae and sit back and bask in the light of admiration.

When made with a warm brownie, this sundae is simply heavenly. We've found the microwave to be the most efficient and effective method of heating the Brownie all the way through, while still retaining its moisture. You may also wrap the Brownie in aluminum foil and bake for 5 minutes in a 300°F oven.

1 Brownie square (page 182)

2 (4-ounce) scoops vanilla ice cream

¼ cup Hot Fudge (page 161)

½ cup Whipped Cream (page 177)

2 tablespoons walnuts, finely chopped (optional)

1 maraschino cherry

Place the Brownie in a beehive bowl off to one side, with a corner pointing down into the center of the bowl. Place the two scoops of ice cream side by side with the Brownie poking up from between them. Drizzle the fudge on the Brownie and around the sides of the ice cream, leaving a "bald spot" for your Whipped Cream. Top with Whipped Cream, walnuts, and the cherry. Serve immediately.

VARIATIONS

The Brownie Sundae has presented itself in numerous guises on our menu as the seasons change. We recommend you have a double scoop of fun inventing brownie sundaes in your own kitchen. Here are some of our favorite combinations to help inspire you. Follow the directions for making a Brownie Sundae, with the following substitutions and toppings.

The Winter Wonderland Substitute mint chocolate chip ice cream for the vanilla ice cream. Substitute crushed candy canes for the walnuts.

The Chocolate Thunder Substitute chocolate ice cream for the vanilla ice cream. Substitute shaved chocolate for the walnuts.

The Raspberry Beret Add ¼ cup Raspberry Compote (page 165). Eliminate the walnuts.

PEANUT BUTTER CUP

As is usually the case in life, the greatest accomplishments are often the result of an honest mistake. Originally, we thought that chocolate would be the ice cream flavor best suited to replicate one of our favorite candies. But after someone inadvertently put a lid labeled "chocolate" on a container of coffee ice cream, we wound up with a coffee ice cream, hot fudge, and peanut butter combination. Two bites in, we realized the "mistake" tasted more like a Reese's Peanut Butter Cup than we could have imagined. This ever-popular sundae features our Peanut Butter, and it's not uncommon for our customers to lick the bowl clean when they get to the bottom of it.

½ cup Peanut Butter (page 174)

2 (4-ounce) scoops coffee ice cream

¼ cup Hot Fudge (page 161)

½ cup Whipped Cream (page 177)

Shaved chocolate

With the back of a soup spoon, smear ¼ cup of the Peanut Butter around the inside of a beehive sundae bowl. Begin in the center of the bowl and, rotating the bowl, work your way up the sides of the bowl to about two-thirds of the way to the top. Place 1 scoop of the ice cream on top of the Peanut Butter in the center of the bowl. Press the second scoop firmly down on top of the first scoop, creating a double stack. Pour the fudge in the "moat" around the sides of the ice cream. Place the remaining dollop of Peanut Butter on top of the ice cream. Top with Whipped Cream and shaved chocolate. Serve immediately.

PECAN CRUMBLE SUNDAE

In the words of Brooklyn native Biggie Smalls, "Mo Money Mo Problems." And in our experience, sometimes more complicated sundaes only result in more complicated preparation—not necessarily a tastier sundae. While the components and preparation of this sundae are simple, its flavor is both complex and deeply satisfying.

1 (4-ounce) scoop chocolate ice cream

½ cup Pecan Oat Crumble (page 157)

1 (4-ounce) scoop vanilla ice cream

¼ cup Caramel Sauce (page 162)

½ cup Whipped Cream (page 177)

2 tablespoons pecans, lightly toasted and finely chopped

Place the scoop of chocolate ice cream in the center of a beehive sundae bowl and sprinkle ¼ cup of the crumble into the "moat" around the ice cream. Press the scoop of vanilla ice cream firmly down on top of the chocolate scoop, creating a double stack. Spread the remaining crumble on top of the ice cream and pour the sauce over all. Top with Whipped Cream and scatter the pecans over the Whipped Cream. Serve immediately.

CLAIMANTS TO THE INVENTION OF THE SUNDAE

Seltzer might be the lifeblood of the fountain, but a lonely life it would have had without ice cream. A counter free of the sticky rings of an ice cream soda and well-licked sundae spoon? Unthinkable. The prominence of these fountain staples are not in dispute. But their origins are.

The ice cream sundae has as many origin stories as it has toppings. One version credits a fountain dispenser in Evanston, Illinois, who, in a clever slip of that town's rather puritanical Blue Laws outlawing the sale of soda on Sundays, happily served ice cream sodas *without* the soda (aka ice cream and soda syrup.)

Another version takes place in Two Rivers, Wisconsin, in 1881: A guy walks into a fountain and asks for ice cream with soda syrup on top. The owner, a savvy businessman named Ed Berners, adds the new dish on the menu and a nickel to its price. Soon Berner's competitors are threatening a price war and negotiations settle on this concession: the new delight will only be sold on Sundays.

Meanwhile, the historians of Ithaca, New York, have staked their own claim, noting that the first mention of an ice cream sundae in print is associated with their own Platt & Colt Pharmacy, where in 1893 Chester Platt fixed a special treat for the Reverend John Scott. It was the good reverend who took a look at this scoop of vanilla ice cream with cherry syrup and a candied cherry on top and named it a Cherry Sunday. There are several newspaper ads as well as some Platt & Colt ledgers to back up their claim. (And they say that Berner fellow in Wisconsin would have only been seventeen in 1881, too young to have engaged in intra-city price-fixing schemes.)

So yes, there are a lot of people wanting a bite of the sundae. As they say, "success has many fathers" (but hot clam soda is an orphan).

As for "sunday" or "sundae"—there is no consensus on which spelling is original or how one became the other. Was it "fancy spelling" for a "fancy drink?" A modest cry against blasphemy? Who knows. But some Missourians of a certain age still call ice cream and hot fudge with whipped cream on top a "sondhi," even if they stopped spelling it that way more than a century ago and don't much care who "invented" it.

MR. POTATO HEAD SUNDAE

MAKES 1 SUNDAE

One of the greatest joys at our soda fountain is bearing witness to the special events that define people's lives. Father's Day is a great example because we have always been Dad's go-to spot to treat his family. (Yes, we know when you're feeding them ice cream for breakfast, Dad!)

When we looked to create a Father's Day sundae, we began by asking ourselves, "What do dads really like?" Our answer: Dads like ice cream. Dads like caramel. Dads like potato chips. Our first try was good, but there was still something missing. So, as a way to hold together the sweetness of the caramel and the saltiness of the potato chip, we added our Peanut Butter smack in the middle of the sundae. Because, after all, what is Dad if not the peanut butter that holds the family together?

1 (4-ounce) scoop vanilla
ice cream

1 (2-ounce) scoop vanilla
ice cream

1 (1-ounce) bag salted kettle-style
potato chips, slightly crushed

¼ cup Peanut Butter (page 174)

¼ cup Caramel Sauce
(page 162)

½ cup Whipped Cream
(page 177)

Place the 4-ounce scoop of ice cream in the center of a beehive sundae bowl. Press the 2-ounce scoop firmly down on top of the first scoop, creating a double stack. Distribute the potato chips in the "moat" around the ice cream. Spoon the Peanut Butter on top of the ice cream. Drizzle the sauce over the Peanut Butter. Top with Whipped Cream. Serve immediately.

BERRY SHORTCAKE CRUMBLE
(aka the Mother of All Sundaes)

MAKES 1 SUNDAE

This "mother of all sundaes" made its original debut on Mother's Day 2011, and was featured that year in *Vogue*. The next summer, we decided to switch it up and developed our Shortcake Crumble for this summertime treat. Our aim was to get everything you love about berry shortcake into *one bite*, and the crumble was the perfect solution. If you do want cake instead of the Shortcake Crumble, try the Vanilla Cakes (page 196). You can also do what we do all summer long as different fruits come into season: swap out the Strawberry Compote for Blueberry Compote (page 166), Blackberry Compote (page 167), Peach Compote (page 170), or Raspberry Compote (page 165).

2 (4-ounce) scoops vanilla
ice cream

½ cup Strawberry Compote
(page 168)

½ cup Shortcake Crumble
(page 159)

¾ cup Whipped Cream
(page 177)

Strawberries, for garnish

Place 1 scoop of the ice cream in the center of a beehive sundae bowl. Press the second scoop firmly down on top of the first scoop, creating a double stack. Spoon the compote over and around the ice cream in the bottom of the bowl, then cover with the cumble. Top with Whipped Cream and garnish with strawberries. Serve immediately.

THE SUNDAE OF BROKEN DREAMS

In Brooklyn, pretzel rods are served with egg creams, and we imagine that it's every pretzel rod's dream to sit proudly on the soda fountain counter. However, the journey to the fountain is rife with danger. Baked, salted, packaged, and shipped off into the unknown, the brittle truth is that not all pretzel dreams are realized. This sad fact was made readily apparent when we received our first delivery of pretzel rods, broken.

A classic American story of rags to riches, perseverance and triumph, the broken pretzel was resurrected in the Sundae of Broken Dreams, alongside vanilla ice cream, swimming in caramel, and blanketed by whipped cream. By popular demand, this sundae has remained on our menu since its debut in 2010 and has been honored by *TimeOutNY* and *New York* on lists of NYC's Top Summer Treats. It is a story (and a sundae) so salty and sweet, you can cry over it.

½ cup broken salted pretzel bits, in pieces no longer than 1 inch

6 tablespoons Caramel Sauce (page 162)

2 (4-ounce) scoops vanilla ice cream

½ cup Whipped Cream (page 177)

Place ¼ cup of the pretzels in the bottom of a beehive sundae bowl and drizzle 3 tablespoons of sauce over them. Place 1 scoop of the ice cream on top of the pretzels in the center of the bowl. Press the second scoop firmly down on top of the first scoop, creating a double stack. Scatter the remaining pretzels over the ice cream and drizzle with the remaining sauce. Top with Whipped Cream and serve immediately.

THE ELVIS

Our sundaes are often described as "decadent." This sundae is a tribute to Elvis Presley because who makes a better flag bearer for decadence than the King himself? Elvis's favorite sandwich was peanut butter, banana, and bacon. So we started with those ingredients, but embellished them by adding caramel and a pickle side. Now that's a sundae fit for a king! If you really, really want to rock out, try substituting Banana Rum Sauce (page 160) for the banana and caramel.

½ cup Peanut Butter
(page 174)

1 (4-ounce) scoop vanilla
ice cream

1 (2-ounce) scoop vanilla
ice cream

1 ripe medium banana, peeled
and sliced in ¼-inch-thick rounds

⅓ cup Caramel Sauce
(page 162)

2 tablespoons Candied
Bacon Bits (page 175)

½ cup Whipped Cream
(page 177)

1 sour pickle spear

With the back of a soup spoon, smear ¼ cup of Peanut Butter around the inside of a beehive sundae bowl. Begin in the center of the bowl and, rotating the bowl, work your way up the sides of the bowl to about two-thirds of the way to the top. Place the 4-ounce scoop of ice cream on top of the Peanut Butter in the center of the bowl. Press the 2-ounce scoop firmly down on top of the first scoop, creating a double stack, maintaining a "moat" around the ice cream (to accommodate your bananas). Put the banana slices in the moat around sides of the ice cream, drizzle with sauce, and scatter the Candied Bacon Bits on top. Spoon the remaining dollop of Peanut Butter on the ice cream. Top with Whipped Cream and scatter bacon bits over. Serve immediately with a pickle side.

CHAPTER ELEVEN

MILKSHAKES

Our milkshakes are handspun and criminally delicious. That's because we put almost a full pint of ice cream in each one and hand spin them in our Hamilton Beach triple spindle to break up the ice cream in the cup as it is mixed. But the heat and the spin of the blades alone don't blend a perfect shake—we have to hunt for lumps too, and you'll likely need to as well. To get a handspun effect at home, start with your blender on low speed to break up the ice cream and work up to a higher speed for the final blend. A great shake is not just thick. It's smooth.

The term "milkshake" was derived from the early practice of shaking a glass of milk, crushed ice, and adding flavoring. Like the ice cream soda, the modern milkshake didn't actually contain ice cream until technology made it an easy mix.

Electric blenders appeared in 1910, promoted largely by the Horlicks Malted Milk Company to make, of course, malted milk. Adding ice cream to that beverage was probably an idea that plenty of soda jerks had, but it is the celebrated jerk Pop Coulson of Walgreen's who gets the everlasting glory as the guy who invented the ice cream milkshake. His innovation was to add two scoops of vanilla ice cream to the standard malted milk drink recipe (milk, chocolate syrup, and malt powder). Soon, there were lines down the block and mixers whirring at each of Walgreen's twenty Chicago soda fountains. Al Capone was a fan. He reportedly liked his with a raw egg, and always left a dollar tip on the twenty-cent drink.

In 1936, the "Multimixer" made its debut, making it feasible for a nimble jerk to mix five shakes at once. The Hamilton Beach is still the gold standard for mixers, and shakes are the genesis of some of the best soda fountain lingo: "Twist it, choke it, and make it cackle" denotes a chocolate malted milkshake with an egg, "shake one in the hay" refers to a strawberry shake, and a "white cow" is a vanilla milkshake.

TOOLS

Blender (or spindle drink mixer)

Ice cream scoops, one 2-ounce
and one 4-ounce

Milkshake (also known as a malt) cup
(for use with a spindle drink mixer,
or served alongside a fountain
glass for presentation)

Fountain glass

Soda spoon

Milkshake straw

CHERRY BLOSSOM SHAKE

MAKES 1 MILKSHAKE

A milkshake inspired by Japanese cherry blossoms. Pretty, pink, and worth waiting for.

2 (4-ounce) scoops vanilla
ice cream

1 (2-ounce) scoop vanilla
ice cream

¼ cup cold whole milk

5 maraschino cherries,
coarsely chopped, plus
1 whole maraschino cherry

¼ cup Whipped Cream
(page 177)

Place the ice cream in the blender jar and pour in the milk. Blend at a low speed for 10 to 15 seconds to break up the ice cream. Increase the blender speed to medium and blend to the desired consistency. Add the cherries and blend just until combined, no more than 3 seconds. (The idea is to simply mix in the cherries, without breaking them down any further.)

Pour into a fountain glass, top with Whipped Cream and a cherry, and serve immediately.

THE ROCKET SHAKE

MAKES 1 MILKSHAKE

This one goes out to all the new parents in our neighborhood, and there are many, who we figured could use another cup of joe (disguised as dessert). Unlike our other milkshakes, this one is designed to be thinner and frothier.

2 (4-ounce) scoops coffee
ice cream

¼ cup strongly brewed
coffee, cold

¼ cup heavy cream

Place the ice cream in the blender jar and pour in the coffee and cream. Blend at a low speed for 10 to 15 seconds to break up the ice cream. Increase the blender speed and blend to the desired consistency.

Pour into a fountain glass and serve immediately.

CLASSIC BLACK-AND-WHITE SHAKE

MAKES 1 MILKSHAKE

There are two versions of a black-and-white milkshake that we serve at the soda fountain. One of them simply calls for a combination of chocolate and vanilla ice cream. But the other one . . . ohhhhh.

2 (4-ounce) scoops vanilla ice cream

1 (2-ounce) scoop vanilla ice cream

¼ cup cold whole milk

¼ cup Hot Fudge (page 161)

Place the ice cream in the blender jar and pour in the milk. Blend at a low speed for 10 to 15 seconds to break up the ice cream. Increase the blender speed to medium and blend to the desired consistency (keeping in mind that a thick milkshake works better for this recipe).

Pour the fudge in three "stripes" down the inside of a fountain glass, allowing the fudge to pool in the bottom of the glass. Gently pour the blended milkshake into the center of the glass (your stripes of fudge should remain intact).

Serve immediately.

VARIATIONS

The Rudolph Shake Substitute peppermint stick ice cream for the vanilla ice cream. Top with ¼ cup Whipped Cream (page 177) and a maraschino cherry.

The Brown-and-White Substitute Caramel Sauce (page 162) for the Hot Fudge.

SEASONAL FRUIT SHAKE

At the height of summer, nothing tastes better than seasonal fruits or berries blended into ice cream. Our seasonal shakes change from week to week at the soda fountain, fully celebrating the bounty of summer.

2 (4-ounce) scoops vanilla ice cream

1 (2-ounce) scoop vanilla ice cream

½ cup compote, any flavor (pages 65–70)

¼ cup Whipped Cream (page 177)

Place the ice cream in the blender jar and blend at a low speed for 10 to 15 seconds to break up the ice cream. Increase the blender speed to medium and blend to the desired consistency. Add the Compote and blend just until combined, no more than 3 seconds. (The idea is simply to mix in the fruit, without breaking it down any further.)

Pour into a fountain glass, top with Whipped Cream, and serve immediately.

SEVEN-LAYER APPLE PARFAIT SHAKE

MAKES 1 MILKSHAKE

New York State apples, in one form or another, make their way onto our menu every autumn. This shake is actually a parfait and involves the deconstruction of the basic components of apple pie à la mode, rebuilt into a layered milkshake treat. While it might be amusing, it would be rather unappetizing to shove a slice of apple pie into a blender, so we created a way to present these beloved ingredients artistically.

Use your eyes to build this parfait, aiming for a balanced series of layers that gracefully ascend to the top of the fountain glass.

2 (4-ounce) scoops vanilla ice cream

3 tablespoons cold whole milk

¾ cup Apple Compote (page 169)

½ cup Pie Crust Crumble (page 152)

¼ cup Whipped Cream (page 177)

Dash of ground cinnamon

Place the ice cream in the blender jar and pour in the milk. Blend the ice cream at a low speed for 10 to 15 seconds to break up the ice cream. Increase the blender speed to medium and blend to the desired consistency.

Put ¼ cup of the compote in the bottom of a fountain glass, then add ¼ cup of the crumble. Spoon the milkshake into the glass until it is just shy of half full. Gently spoon in another ¼ cup of the compote, taking care not to mix it with the lower layers of the parfait. Add the remaining milkshake, leaving 1 inch of empty space to the top of the glass. Add the remaining compote, then the remaining crumble.

Top with Whipped Cream and dust with cinnamon. Serve immediately.

PECAN PIE BAR SHAKE

MAKES 1 MILKSHAKE

This is a truly delicious mash-up that spotlights one of our favorites, the Pecan Pie Bar. If you like pecan pie with a scoop of vanilla ice cream, it goes without saying that you'll love this shake.

2 (4-ounce) scoops vanilla ice cream

1 (2-ounce) scoop vanilla ice cream

¼ cup cold whole milk

1 Pecan Pie Bar (page 183), coarsely chopped

¼ cup Whipped Cream (page 177)

1 tablespoon lightly toasted pecans, finely chopped

Place the ice cream in the blender jar and pour in the milk. Blend at a low speed for 10 to 15 seconds to break up the ice cream. Increase the blender speed to medium and blend to desired consistency. Add the Pecan Pie Bar and blend just until combined, no more than 3 seconds. (The idea is to simply mix in the Pecan Pie Bar, without breaking it down any further.) Pour into a fountain glass.

Top with Whipped Cream and scatter with pecans. Serve immediately.

PEANUT BUTTER SHAKE

MAKES 1 MILKSHAKE

Our Peanut Butter (page 174) has fans far and wide. Adding it to a milkshake just makes a good thing better.

2 (4-ounce) scoops vanilla or chocolate ice cream

1 (2-ounce) scoop vanilla or chocolate ice cream

¼ cup cold whole milk

¼ cup Peanut Butter (page 174)

Place the ice cream in the blender jar and blend at a low speed for 10 to 15 seconds to break up the ice cream. Increase the blender speed to medium and blend to the desired consistency. Add the Peanut Butter and blend just until combined, no more than 3 seconds. (The idea is to simply mix in the Peanut Butter.)

Pour into a fountain glass and serve immediately.

SODA SHAKE

On a hot day in July, we served a kid a milkshake. "How was it?" we asked when he finished. "Great. But now I'm thirsty." Say hello to the Soda Shake. Why? 'Cause you're thirsty after you drink a shake. Thanks, kid.

This is an opportunity to release your inner soda jerk with the nifty trick of floating a milkshake on top of a soda. If anyone asks, tell 'em it's magic.

6 tablespoons soda syrup, any flavor (pages 59–79)

1¼ cups plain cold seltzer

2 (4-ounce) scoops vanilla ice cream

1 (2-ounce) scoop vanilla ice cream

¼ cup cold whole milk

Pour the syrup into a small pitcher, add the seltzer, and stir gently just until combined. Pour equal amounts into two separate fountain glasses and keep chilled until ready to use.

Place the ice cream in the blender jar and pour in the milk. Blend the ice cream at a low speed for 10 to 15 seconds to break up the ice cream. Increase the blender speed to medium and blend to the desired consistency (keeping in mind that a thick milkshake works better for this recipe).

Gently pour the milkshake onto the soda, one glass at a time, while holding a soda spoon inside the glass to serve as a brake so that the milkshake doesn't sink into the soda. Initially, fizzing will occur when the fat in the shake meets the carbonation in the soda. But, once you've got a 1-inch milkshake seal on top of the soda, you can safely pour in the remaining milkshake to achieve the desired effect. Serve immediately.

CHAPTER TWELVE

TOPPINGS

If clothes make the man, then toppings make the sundae. It's hard to beat a good-old unadulterated traditional sundae, but at the Farmacy we like trying. Crumbles, sauces and compotes, and nut butters—we couldn't make our sundaes without them, and we'd be at a loss for sundae names. Where do you think we got the Cookie Monster and the Almond Joyful? Although a good coconut crumble or a spoonful of Nutty-Ella can easily stand alone (and frequently does as a late-night staff snack once we've closed the fountain), put them together over ice cream and . . . bliss.

CRUMBLES

A few of these crumbles can be made into cookies like the Chocolate Chip (page 154) and the Hot Mama (page 156), if you prefer them without the ice cream. Or, you can just fill a bowl with them and eat them with a spoon.

PIE CRUST CRUMBLE

MAKES ABOUT 4 CUPS

An easy recipe to make if you have an unbaked pie crust on hand, this one makes a sublime sundae with vanilla ice cream and any kind of fruit compote. Try Apple Compote (page 169) or Blackberry (page 167), Blueberry (page 166), Peach (page 170), Raspberry (page 165), or Strawberry Compote (page 168). This crumble is featured in the Seven-Layer Apple Parfait Shake (page 147).

One recipe Pie Crust (page 198)

Preheat the oven to 375°F.

On a lightly floured surface, roll out the pie crust to an even ¼ inch thick. Transfer it to a nonstick baking sheet (or cut it to fit on 2 sheets, if necessary) and freeze for 15 minutes. Bake the crumble until uniformly golden brown, about 25 minutes. Cool completely in the pan on a wire rack. When it's cool, use your fingers to break up the crumble into bite-sized pieces 1 inch or smaller.

Store in a covered plastic container at room temperature for up to 3 days or frozen for up to 3 months. If frozen, allow to thaw in the refrigerator overnight before serving.

AMAZING GRAHAM CRUMBLE

MAKES ABOUT 4 CUPS

Graham flour can easily be found in health food stores in the baking section along with all the other flours. Contrary to what you might think, it's just whole wheat flour, but it's milled in a very specific way. It's named for a nineteenth-century Presbyterian minister, Sylvester Graham, who advocated the use of whole grain wheat flour instead of the crummy white stuff that gained popularity during the Industrial Revolution. This crumble is featured in the Doris Seymour sundae (page 115).

1 cup plus 2 tablespoons (5.7 ounces) all-purpose flour

¼ cup plus 2 tablespoons (2 ounces) graham flour

⅓ cup (2.3 ounces) firmly packed light brown sugar

¼ teaspoon sea salt

¾ cup (6 ounces) unsalted butter, browned and cooled to room temperature (see page 157)

3 tablespoons (2.3 ounces) honey

Preheat the oven to 325°F.

Combine the flours, sugar, and salt in a bowl. In a separate bowl, combine the butter and honey and pour the mixture over the dry ingredients, mixing thoroughly with a rubber spatula. Put the dough on a nonstick rimmed baking sheet and pat it down to a thickness of ⅛ inch. (While you can use your rubber spatula to do this, it's easier just to use your fingers to push the dough out toward the edges of the pan and then make everything level with the flat of your hand.) Use a fork to rake parallel furrows in the dough, first in one direction and then at a 90-degree angle to the first set of furrows. (When you're done it should look like a length of dirt road after a hard rain.) Place in the freezer for 10 minutes before baking.

Bake the crumble until golden brown, 15 to 20 minutes. Let cool completely in the pan on a wire rack. When it's cool, use your fingers to break up the crumble into bite-sized pieces 1 inch or smaller.

Store in a covered plastic container at room temperature for up to 3 days or frozen for up to 3 months. If frozen, allow to thaw in the refrigerator overnight before serving.

VARIATION

Chocolate-Covered Graham Chunks
Sprinkle 1 cup (6 ounces) of semisweet chocolate chips over the still-hot surface of the Amazing Graham Crumble as soon as it's pulled from the oven. Let the chocolate sit for 5 minutes until it's melted and then spread it over the crumble with a rubber spatula. Sprinkle ½ teaspoon of sea salt over the surface (totally optional) and refrigerate. When it's firm, break it up into chunks of any size. Store as directed above.

MAKES ABOUT 1½ POUNDS

CHOCOLATE CHIP COOKIE CRUMBLE

MAKES ABOUT 4 CUPS

Kids adore this crumble, so it's a good one to serve at birthday parties and sleepovers. Shoot, why not have the kids help make it? Breaking up the baked crumble is an activity any kid can get into. (We love this part too, and we're grown-ups!) This crumble is featured in the Cookie Monster sundae (page 118).

⅓ cup (2.3 ounces) firmly packed light brown sugar

3 tablespoons (1.5 ounces) cane sugar

½ cup plus 2 tablespoons (5 ounces) unsalted butter, browned and cooled to room temperature (see page 157)

1 large egg, slightly beaten

1 teaspoon pure vanilla extract

1 cup (5 ounces) all-purpose flour

¼ teaspoon baking soda

¼ teaspoon sea salt

½ cup (3 ounces) semisweet chocolate chips

Preheat the oven to 325°F.

Combine the sugars in a bowl, pour the butter over them and mix thoroughly with a rubber spatula. Add the egg and vanilla and mix in thoroughly. In a separate bowl, combine the flour, baking soda, and salt, and stir with a fork to combine. Add the dry ingredients to the wet and mix just until the dough is uniformly combined. Mix in the chocolate chips.

Put the dough on a nonstick rimmed baking sheet and use a rubber spatula to spread it out to a thickness of ½ inch, making it as level as possible. Freeze the dough for 10 minutes before baking.

Bake the crumble until uniformly golden brown, about 30 minutes, rotating the pan halfway through the baking time. Cool completely in the pan on a wire rack. When it's cool, use your fingers to break up the crumble into bite-sized pieces 1 inch or smaller.

Store in a covered plastic container at room temperature for up to 3 days or frozen for up to 3 months. If frozen, allow to thaw in the refrigerator overnight before serving.

VARIATION

Chocolate Chip Cookies Drop generous tablespoons of dough onto a nonstick baking sheet 2 inches apart, and flatten to 2-inch rounds. Bake at 400°F until the center of the cookies is set, about 8 minutes. Let the cookies cool on the sheet before removing. Cookies may be stored in a plastic covered container at room temperature for up to 3 days. Unbaked cookie dough may be stored frozen in a covered plastic container for up to 3 months. Allow frozen dough to thaw overnight in the refrigerator before baking.

MAKES ABOUT 12 COOKIES

COCONUT ALMOND MACAROON CRUMBLE

Almond flour, a common ingredient in European pastry, can be found in specialty food stores and health food stores in the baking section. Watch closely while you're toasting the coconut and almonds—they can go from toasted to burned in the blink of an eye. This crumble is featured in the Almond Joyful sundae (page 114).

⅓ cup (1.3 ounces) slivered almonds

¼ cup (0.8 ounce) sweetened shredded coconut

¾ cup plus 1 tablespoon (4.1 ounces) all-purpose flour

½ cup plus 1 tablespoon (1.9 ounces) almond flour

½ cup (4 ounces) cane sugar

½ cup plus 1 tablespoon (4.5 ounces) unsalted butter, melted and cooled to room temperature (see page 157)

¼ teaspoon pure almond extract

¼ teaspoon pure coconut extract

2 teaspoons honey

Preheat the oven to 350°F.

Spread the almonds out on a rimmed baking sheet and toast in the oven for 3 minutes. Remove the pan from the oven, stir the almonds, and then sprinkle the coconut on top. Return to the oven and toast for an additional 3 minutes, stirring at the halfway point. Remove from the oven and set aside to cool. Increase the oven temperature to 400°F.

Combine the almonds, coconut, flours, and sugar in a bowl. In a separate bowl, combine the butter, extracts, and honey and mix thoroughly. Pour the wet ingredients over the dry ingredients and mix thoroughly with a rubber spatula. Put the dough on a nonstick rimmed baking sheet and spread it out with your fingers, separating and breaking up larger clumps so they're no bigger than 2 inches in diameter. There will be gaps in the dough through which you can see the metal of the pan. Freeze for 10 minutes before baking.

Bake the crumble until golden brown around the edges, about 10 minutes. Cool completely in the pan on a wire rack. When it's cool, use your fingers to break up the crumble into bite-sized pieces 1 inch or smaller.

Store in a covered plastic container at room temperature for up to 3 days or frozen for up to 3 months. If frozen, allow to thaw in the refrigerator overnight before serving.

HOT MAMA CRUMBLE

While this was developed as a crumble topping for the Hot Mama sundae (page 124) on Mother's Day, it's a great stand-alone cookie. If it's too spicy, dial down the cayenne.

¾ cup (3.8 ounces) all-purpose flour

¼ cup (1 ounce) Dutch-processed cocoa powder

½ teaspoon baking soda

¼ teaspoon salt

¾ teaspoon ground cinnamon

¼ teaspoon cayenne pepper (plus ⅛ teaspoon more if you want your crumble to have more bite)

½ cup (4 ounces) unsalted butter, at room temperature

½ cup (4 ounces) cane sugar

½ teaspoon pure vanilla extract

¼ cup (0.9 ounce) rolled oats

⅓ cup (2 ounces) semisweet chocolate chips

Preheat the oven to 350°F.

In a bowl, combine the flour, cocoa, baking soda, salt, cinnamon, and cayenne, and stir with a fork to combine. Set aside.

In the bowl of an electric mixer fitted with the paddle attachment or in a large bowl and using a wooden spoon, cream the butter until smooth; add the sugar and vanilla and mix thoroughly. Add the dry ingredients to the butter mixture and stir. Mix in the oats, then the chocolate chips.

Put the dough on a nonstick rimmed baking sheet and spread it out with your fingers, separating and breaking up larger clumps so they're no bigger than 2 inches in diameter. There will be gaps in the dough through which you can see the metal of the pan. Freeze for 10 minutes before baking.

Bake the crumble until cracks begin to appear in the top of the dough, about 14 minutes. Cool completely in the pan on a wire rack. When it's cool, use your fingers to break up the crumble into bite-sized pieces 1 inch or smaller.

Store in a plastic covered container at room temperature for up to 3 days or frozen for up to 3 months. If frozen, allow to thaw in the refrigerator overnight before serving.

VARIATION

Hot Mama Cookies Drop generous tablespoons of dough onto a nonstick cookie sheet and flatten to 2-inch rounds, spaced 2 inches apart. Bake at 350°F until cracks appear in the tops of the cookies, about 14 minutes. Let the cookies cool on the sheet before removing. Cookies may be stored in a plastic covered container at room temperature for up to 3 days. Unbaked cookie dough may be stored frozen in a covered plastic container for up to 3 months. Allow frozen dough to thaw overnight in the refrigerator before baking.

MAKES ABOUT 12 COOKIES

PECAN OAT CRUMBLE

MAKES ABOUT 4 CUPS

When we created this crumble, we were going for the taste and texture of pecan sandies. The brown rice flour complements the pecans and, because it's gluten free, lends a nice sandy texture. Brown rice flour can be found in the baking section of most health food stores. This crumble is featured in the Pecan Crumble sundae (page 130).

¾ cup (3.8 ounces) all-purpose flour

2 tablespoons (0.7 ounce) brown rice flour

⅓ cup plus 1 tablespoon (2.8 ounces) firmly packed light brown sugar

¼ cup (0.9 ounce) rolled oats

½ cup (2 ounces) pecan halves, coarsely chopped

¼ teaspoon sea salt

½ cup (4 oz.) unsalted butter, browned and cooled to room temperature (see below)

½ teaspoon vanilla bean paste

Preheat the oven to 400°F.

Combine the flours, sugar, oats, pecans, and salt in a bowl and stir with a fork to combine. In a separate bowl, combine the butter and vanilla bean paste and pour them over the dry ingredients, mixing thoroughly with a rubber spatula. Empty the dough onto a nonstick rimmed baking sheet and spread it out with your fingers. There will be gaps in the dough through which you can see the metal of the pan. Freeze for 10 minutes before baking.

Bake the crumble until it is just beginning to brown, about 10 minutes. Cool completely in the pan on a wire rack. When it's cool, use your fingers to break up the crumble into bite-sized pieces 1 inch or smaller. (This crumble should be "sandy," so don't completely pulverize it.)

Store in a covered plastic container at room temperature for up to 3 days or frozen for up to 3 months. If frozen, allow to thaw in the refrigerator overnight before serving.

TIPS FOR BROWNING BUTTER

Here's a tutorial on how to make nutty brown butter. Melt the butter over medium heat in a saucepan that's a little larger than you think you'll need. Bring to a boil and then keep it at a steady boil until it browns. It will go through a few stages, at one point foaming. Keep a close eye on it after the foam subsides. It's done when the milk solids have separated from the fats and gathered on the bottom of the saucepan, turning the color of toasted bread crumbs, and it smells toasted and nutty. How long this takes depends on the amount of butter you're browning and the size of your pan, so it's best to rely on your eyes and nose to tell you when it's done. Be careful not to overcook the butter, or the milk solids will burn and give the butter an acrid flavor.

PISTACHIO CRUMBLE

MAKES ABOUT 4 CUPS

Pistachio paste is the same as almond paste, except it features pistachios. In Brooklyn, it's pretty easy to find since it's made by the American Almond Products Co. located in the Bedford-Stuyvesant neighborhood of Brooklyn. If you don't have access to a supermarket with a really good specialty foods selection, you may need to purchase pistachio paste online. The same goes for rose water, though you will most definitely find it in stores that cater to people from the Middle East. This crumble is featured in Simi's Sundae (page 123).

¾ cup plus 1 tablespoon (4.1 ounces) all-purpose flour

½ cup plus 1 tablespoon (4.5 ounces) cane sugar

½ cup (5.5 ounces) pistachio paste

¼ teaspoon rose water (optional)

¾ cup (6 ounces) cold unsalted butter, cut in ½-inch cubes

⅓ cup (1.5 ounces) shelled pistachios

Preheat the oven to 375°F.

Combine the flour, sugar, and pistachio paste in a bowl. Incorporate the pistachio paste into the dry ingredients by rubbing the mixture with your fingertips. If you're using rose water, sprinkle it over the mixture. Add the butter and cut it in with a pastry cutter or two knives, stopping when the butter has been reduced to pea-size, or smaller, bits. Mix in the pistachios with a fork. Empty the dough onto a nonstick rimmed baking sheet and spread it out with your fingers, separating and breaking up larger clumps so they're no bigger than 2 inches in diameter. There will be gaps in the dough through which you can see the metal of the pan. Freeze for 10 minutes before baking.

Bake the crumble until the edges have started to turn golden brown, about 10 minutes. Cool completely in the pan on a wire rack. When it's cool, use your fingers to break up the crumble into bite-sized pieces 1 inch or smaller.

Store in a covered plastic container at room temperature for up to 3 days or frozen for up to 3 months. If frozen, allow to thaw in the refrigerator overnight before serving.

SHORTCAKE CRUMBLE

This salty-sweet crumble began its journey into a sundae by way of a scone that we were developing for brunch. Versatile and irresistible, it's a breeze to throw together and smell divine while baking. This crumble is featured in the Berry Shortcake Crumble sundae (page 134).

2 cups (10 ounces) all-purpose flour

1 tablespoon baking powder

½ teaspoon baking soda

½ teaspoon sea salt

6 tablespoons (3 ounces) cold unsalted butter, cut in ½-inch cubes

1 large egg

½ cup (4 ounces) buttermilk

2 tablespoons (0.9 ounce) firmly packed light brown sugar

1 teaspoon pure vanilla extract

Preheat the oven to 400°F.

Combine the flour, baking powder, baking soda, and salt in a large bowl and stir with a fork. Cut the butter into the dry ingredients with a pastry cutter or two knives until the mixture is the texture of coarsely ground cornmeal with a smattering of peas in it. (You want to do this quickly so your butter doesn't melt. It's okay if there are small lumps of butter in the mixture when you're done.)

In a separate small bowl, briefly whisk the egg. Add the buttermilk and whisk to combine. Then add the brown sugar, rubbing it between your fingers to squash any recalcitrant lumps; add the vanilla extract and whisk again. Make a depression in the center of the dry ingredients and empty the wet ingredients into it. Stir with a fork, reaching to the bottom of the bowl, and mix gently just until the ingredients are combined. (Don't overdo this or your crumble will be tough.)

Empty the dough onto a nonstick rimmed baking sheet and spread it out with your fingers, separating and breaking up larger clumps so they're no bigger than 2 inches in diameter. There will be gaps in the dough through which you can see the metal of the pan.

Bake the crumble until golden brown, 12 to 15 minutes. Cool completely in the pan on a wire rack. When it's cool, use your fingers to break up the crumble into bite-sized pieces 1 inch or smaller.

Store in a covered plastic container at room temperature for up to 1 day or frozen for up to 3 months. If frozen, allow to thaw in the refrigerator overnight before serving.

SAUCES AND COMPOTES

For the wow factor they provide, sauces are relatively easy to make. Buy ripe fruit in season at a farmers' market, find the tastiest honey, splurge on the best chocolate. All of the fruit-based compotes in this book freeze beautifully, so don't be afraid to stock up on fruits while they are in season. In January, you may have the chance to relive a summer day by simply pulling a container of blueberry compote out of the freezer.

BANANA RUM SAUCE

MAKES 1½ CUPS

This boozy sauce is definitely not one for the kiddos, but oh is it tasty! Make it with a good quality dark rum like Myers's, Gosling's Black Seal, or The Kraken Black Spiced Rum. It's recommended in the Elvis sundae (page 138).

4 tablespoons (2 ounces) unsalted butter

1 teaspoon all-purpose flour

3½ tablespoons dark rum

½ cup (3.5 ounces) firmly packed light brown sugar

1 teaspoon pure vanilla extract

2 small to medium ripe bananas (about 9 ounces), mashed to a paste

Melt the butter in a small saucepan over low heat and whisk in the flour. Cook, stirring constantly, for about 1 minute, or until the mixture thickens slightly. Whisk in the rum and cook for 3 minutes, stirring constantly. Add the sugar and cook, stirring constantly, until the sugar dissolves, about 3 minutes. Remove from the heat and whisk in the vanilla and mashed banana, mixing thoroughly. Serve immediately. This sauce is best the day it's made and, since it's a breeze to put together, we recommend making only what you plan to serve right away.

HOT FUDGE

Fudge is as fudge does. And our fudge does a lot. It's one of our most ordered sauces and the backbone of the Anyday Sundae (page 111). It's thick enough to line a fountain glass for the Classic Black-and-White Shake (page 144), and smooth enough to be the base for a cup of hot chocolate.

Semisweet chocolate chips may be substituted for the bittersweet chips in this recipe, but we prefer a darker chocolate. Chopped chocolate bars (in the 70 percent range) can be used if you can't find darker chips. Splurge on good chocolate and cocoa powder and you will be cooing over your hot fudge.

1 cup (8 ounces) water

½ cup (2 ounces) Dutch-processed cocoa powder

1 cup (6 ounces) bittersweet chocolate chips or chopped dark chocolate

1 cup (8 ounces) unsalted butter, cut in 16 pieces

1 cup plus 2 tablespoons (9 ounces) cane sugar

½ cup (6 ounces) honey

1 teaspoon pure vanilla extract

⅛ teaspoon sea salt

Put the 1 cup water and cocoa powder in a saucepan and whisk to combine. Add the chocolate and cook over low heat, whisking often, until the chocolate has melted. Take care during this step as the mixture has a tendency to scorch if it comes to a boil, imparting a slightly burned taste to the final product. As soon as the chocolate has melted, add the butter, 3 or 4 pieces at a time, whisking the fudge for 10 to 15 seconds after each addition. Whisk in the sugar and honey and bring to a slow boil over low heat. Cook 15 minutes, or to desired consistency, whisking occasionally. (Bear in mind that the hot fudge will be much "fudgier" once it's cooled.) Whisk in the vanilla and salt.

Store the topping in glass jars or in covered plastic containers in the refrigerator for up to 2 weeks.

CARAMEL SAUCE

Deeply flavorful and subtly salty, we have to stop ourselves from slathering our Caramel Sauce on everything. As a topping for our sundaes, it's a no-brainer, but try adding this sauce to a mug of warm milk, or to your coffee. While you can use your eyes to gauge whether or not your caramel is done, it's helpful and reassuring to have a candy thermometer on hand for this recipe.

1 cup (8 ounces) water

3 cups (24 ounces) cane sugar

¼ cup (3 ounces) honey

1½ cups (12 ounces) heavy cream

½ cup (4 ounces) unsalted butter, cut into 16 pieces

1½ teaspoons pure vanilla extract

½ teaspoon sea salt

Pour the 1 cup water into a heavy saucepan with high sides and then pour the sugar carefully into the center of the pan. (You don't want the sugar crystals anywhere but in the water or they will make your caramel crystallize.) Then add the honey and bring to a boil, uncovered, over medium heat. Don't stir! (Resist the temptation or you will have a crystallized mess on your hands.) Cook until the mixture is a rich amber color and registers 305°F on your candy thermometer, 10 to 15 minutes. If scum rises to the surface of the caramel while it is cooking, simply skim it off with a spoon from time to time.

Immediately remove the pan from the heat and add ½ cup of the heavy cream. The hot caramel will spit viciously when you add the cream, so stand back and give it a few seconds to calm down; whisk it and then add the remaining cream. Whisk to combine thoroughly and then start adding the butter, 3 or 4 pieces at a time, whisking the caramel after each addition. You don't have to wait for the butter to melt completely between additions, but you want to add the butter slowly enough to successfully incorporate it into the sauce, so whisk for 10 to 15 seconds between additions. After the butter is completely incorporated into the sauce, whisk in the vanilla and salt.

Store the topping in glass jars or covered plastic containers in the refrigerator for up to 2 weeks.

AWESOME CHOCOLATE SHELL

MAKES 2 CUPS

We have the wicked smart folks at *Cook's Illustrated* to thank for this recipe. We'd been scratching our heads about how to make a chocolate sauce that would harden upon hitting ice cream when *Cook's Illustrated* gave us the answer in a response to a reader's letter.

Coconut oil is readily found in health food stores. Just make sure you're buying an edible version, not one specified for use in personal care. Note that it is measured in volume because it's an oil, even though it's solid at room temperature. Do not put Awesome Shell in the refrigerator or you will have to chisel it out of the container! This topping is featured in the Affugazi Affogato sundae (page 112).

2 cups (12 ounces) semisweet chocolate chips

1 cup (8 ounces) coconut oil

Combine the ingredients in a microwavable bowl and microwave at 50 percent power until the chocolate chips have melted, about 1 minute. Stir well to combine. Let cool to room temperature before using.

Store in covered glass jars or plastic containers at room temperature for up to 2 weeks.

RASPBERRY COMPOTE

MAKES ABOUT 4 CUPS

Another reason to celebrate summer, our Raspberry Compote is tart and sweet. Spoon it on a pile of pancakes and make everyone happy at the breakfast table. This compote is featured in the Berry Shortcake Crumble sundae (page 134) and Seasonal Fruit Shake (page 146).

3 pints fresh raspberries, or 36 ounces frozen raspberries

½ cup plus 1 tablespoon (4½ ounces) cane sugar, or more depending on the tartness of the berries

2 teaspoons freshly squeezed lemon juice

2 teaspoons honey

Set aside 1 pint raspberries. Put the remaining raspberries, sugar, and lemon juice in a saucepan and bring to a boil over medium heat. Decrease the heat and simmer, uncovered, for 5 minutes. Remove from the heat and add the honey and the reserved 1 pint raspberries, stirring to combine.

Store the compote in covered glass jars or plastic containers in the refrigerator for up to 2 weeks. The compote may also be frozen in plastic containers for up to 3 months. If frozen, allow to thaw in the refrigerator overnight before serving.

BLUEBERRY COMPOTE

MAKES ABOUT 4 CUPS

Kerplink. Kerplank. Kerplunk. The sounds of blueberries dropping into a tin bucket. When this berry compote hits our menu, we know we are in full summer stride, even if we're not on the coast of Maine. This topping is featured in the Berry Shortcake Crumble sundae (page 134) and the Seasonal Fruit Shake (page 146), but it's also yummy on pancakes or stirred into plain yogurt.

3 pints fresh blueberries, or 36 ounces frozen blueberries

½ cup plus 1 tablespoon (4½ ounces) cane sugar, or more depending on the tartness of the berries

½ cup (4 ounces) water

1 teaspoon freshly squeezed lemon juice

Set aside 1 pint of the blueberries. Put the remaining blueberries, sugar, and the ½ cup water in a saucepan and bring to a boil over medium heat. Decrease the heat and let simmer, uncovered, until the berries burst, about 10 minutes. Remove from the heat and add the lemon juice and reserved 1 pint of blueberries. Let sit, covered, at room temperature for 15 minutes. Uncover and using a potato (or bean) masher, mash the compote in the saucepan 10 times.

Store the topping in covered glass jars or plastic containers in the refrigerator for up to two weeks. This compote may also be frozen, in plastic containers, for up to three months. If frozen, allow to thaw in the refrigerator overnight before serving.

BLACKBERRY COMPOTE

Collecting blackberries in the wild is always a thorny proposition. Thankfully, we have a plethora of farmers' markets that provide plump fresh berries during the summer, but this sauce is just as great with frozen berries. This topping is featured in the Berry Shortcake Crumble sundae (page 134) and the Seasonal Fruit Shake (page 146).

3 pints fresh blackberries, or 30 ounces frozen blackberries

¼ cup plus 2 tablespoons (3 ounces) cane sugar, or more depending on the tartness of the berries

¼ cup (2 ounces) water

1 teaspoon freshly squeezed lime juice

1 teaspoon honey

Set aside ½ cup of the blackberries. Put the remaining blackberries, sugar, and the ¼ cup water in a saucepan and bring to a boil over medium heat. Decrease the heat and let simmer, uncovered for 10 minutes. Remove from the heat and add the the lime juice, honey, and the remaining ½ cup of the blackberries. Using a potato (or bean) masher, mash the compote in the saucepan 5 times.

Store the topping in covered glass jars or plastic containers in the refrigerator for up to two weeks. The compote may also be frozen, in covered plastic containers, for up to three months. If frozen, allow to thaw in the refrigerator overnight before serving.

STRAWBERRY COMPOTE

Strawberries at the peak of season (especially if bought directly from the farmer) are tastier and juicier and will give up more liquid than those bought in a supermarket. Supermarket strawberries have been bred for ease of shipping, not texture or taste. One of the very first things we did upon opening Brooklyn Farmacy in June of 2010 was drive out to the North Fork of Long Island to buy flats of strawberries from Clark McCombe. As many would tell you, no excursion to this area is complete without a side trip to his Briermere Farms for a fresh fruit pie. You need only taste the fruit he grows to understand why Clark's pies are so darn good. This topping is featured in the Berry Shortcake Crumble sundae (page 134) and the Seasonal Fruit Shake (page 146).

4 quarts fresh strawberries, or 5 pounds frozen strawberries

1¾ cups plus 2 tablespoons (15 ounces) cane sugar, or more depending on the tartness of the berries

2 teaspoons freshly squeezed lemon juice

Wash and hull the strawberries, discarding any that are bad and cutting away soft spots as necessary. Cut larger berries in halves or quarters, so that all berries are in pieces no bigger than 1 inch. Set aside one-fourth of the berries. Place the remaining berries and sugar in a large pot, stir, cover, and let sit at room temperature for 15 minutes. (This will draw the juice out of the berries.) Bring the berries to a boil over medium-high heat, decrease the heat to medium-low and simmer for 5 minutes. Remove from the heat and, using a potato (or bean) masher, mash the compote in the saucepan 15 times. Add the remaining berries and the lemon juice. Let cool 15 minutes before proceeding to the next step.

Place a strainer over a large bowl and pour the berry mixture into it in manageable batches, stirring to release the liquid. What's left in the strainer is your Strawberry Compote. The liquid in the bowl is Strawberry Syrup (page 77). Voilà, you just made two recipes in one!

Store the compote and syrup in covered glass jars or plastic containers in the refrigerator for up to 2 weeks. The compote and syrup may also be frozen in plastic containers for up to 3 months. If frozen, allow to thaw in the refrigerator overnight before serving.

APPLE COMPOTE

Any recipe featuring apples is made better when you use a variety of different apples. Apples are the state fruit of New York and gobs of them are grown here. We love going to the farmers' market in October to visit Farmer Fred, whose family has been farming the same land in the Hudson Valley since 1855. His Wilklow Orchards grows an astounding variety of apples with names like Winter Banana, Cameo, and Opalescent. It's featured in the Seven-Layer Apple Parfait Shake (page 147).

2 medium lemons

2 teaspoons ground cinnamon

½ teaspoon ground allspice

¼ teaspoon ground cloves

4 pounds apples, peeled, cored, and cut into ¾-inch dice

1 cup (8 ounces) cane sugar

3 tablespoons (1½ ounces) unsalted butter, cut in 3 pieces

Preheat the oven to 350°F.

Zest part of 1 lemon and put ¼ teaspoon of the zest in a small bowl. Combine the cinnamon, allspice, and cloves with the zest and set the mixture aside.

Juice both lemons and put the juice in a large bowl. Put the diced apples in the bowl with the lemon juice and toss to coat. Sprinkle the spice mixture and sugar over the apples and mix thoroughly with a rubber spatula.

Put the butter on a 10 by 15 by 1-inch rimmed baking sheet and place in the oven just long enough to melt the butter. Put the apples on the buttered pan and stir. Bake for 5 minutes, stir, and then bake until the juices are slightly thickened and caramelized, about 5 minutes more.

Store the compote in covered glass jars or plastic containers in the refrigerator for up to two weeks. The compote may also frozen, in plastic containers, for up to three months. If frozen, allow to thaw in the refrigerator overnight before serving.

PEACH COMPOTE

If it's peach season (August in our neck of the woods) and you're making this sauce with those perfectly ripe peaches you just bought straight from the farmer, then prepare yourself for a sweet experience. This compote is really the best when made in season. The easiest way to peel a peach, which works best with ripe peaches, is to first scald it in boiling water for 10 seconds. Watch your fingers while slicing because peaches are slippery little buggers once their skins come off. This topping is featured in the Berry Shortcake Crumble sundae (page 134) and Seasonal Fruit Shake (page 146).

⅔ cup (4 ounces) water

4 teaspoons amaretto liqueur, or ¼ teaspoon pure almond extract

4 teaspoons apricot preserves

4 teaspoons honey

¼ cup (2 ounces) cane sugar

2 pounds ripe peaches, peeled, pitted, and cut into ¼-inch-thick slices

2 blackberries, for color (optional)

Combine the water, amaretto, apricot preserves, honey, and sugar in a saucepan; drop in the peach slices. Add the blackberries, if you're using them, to the saucepan and bring the peach mixture to a boil over medium heat. Decrease the heat and simmer until the peaches are tender, 15 to 20 minute. With a fork, mash the cooked blackberries against the inside of the saucepan to break them down, then stir them into the peaches.

Store the compote in covered glass jars or plastic containers in the refrigerator for up to 2 weeks. This compote may also be frozen, in plastic containers for up to 3 months. If frozen, allow to thaw in the refrigerator overnight before serving.

MARINATED PINEAPPLE

Just a note to those of you who don't read through the entire recipe before beginning to make it: Start this one the day before you want to serve it. It's called Marinated Pineapple for a reason! This topping is featured in the Flyin' Hawaiian sundae (page 122).

2 cups (16 ounces) cane sugar

1 cup (8 ounces) water

1 ripe medium pineapple, peeled, cored, and cut into ½-inch cubes

1 teaspoon freshly squeezed lemon juice

Combine the sugar and the 1 cup water in a large bowl. Stir the pineapple and lemon juice into the sugar water mixture. Cover with plastic wrap and refrigerate for 24 hours, stirring on occasion, until the sugar has dissolved. If at the end of 24 hours there is still residual sugar at the bottom of the bowl, use a rubber spatula to loosen it and then stir vigorously until the sugar dissolves.

Strain the mixture over a bowl, reserving the liquid. What's left in the strainer is your Marinated Pineapple. The liquid in the bowl is Pineapple Syrup (page 75). Voilà, you just made two recipes in one!

Store the compote in covered glass jars or plastic containers in the refrigerator for up to 2 weeks. The pineapple may also be frozen, in plastic containers for up to 3 months. If frozen, allow to thaw in the refrigerator overnight before serving.

NUT BUTTERS

Delicious nut butters are a breeze to make at home if you have to have a food processor to do it. Unless you have a blender with a monster motor like a Vitamix (see Resources, page 206), most home blenders just can't handle nuts. If you don't have a food processor, buy a good-quality natural nut butter instead. Try a health food store, which will have a more comprehensive selection, or even ones that are freshly ground.

Fresh nuts and nut oils will make exceptional nut butters. We are incredibly lucky to be located mere blocks from the Sahadi Importing Co. where we buy all of our nuts for our nut butters. The origins of Sahadi's go back more than one hundred years and the present incarnation has anchored the same block of Atlantic Avenue since 1948. Charlie Sahadi has been a champion of Brooklyn Farmacy from the beginning. Even when we were at our most tender and green, Charlie took us seriously and assured us a steady supply of the best nuts he could source.

Note that the oils we use are all made from roasted nuts. We do that because of the depth of flavor roasting imparts to nuts. Roasted nut oils can be found in the oil section of well-stocked specialty or health food stores.

ALMOND BUTTER

MAKES ABOUT 4 CUPS

This is a fairly stiff nut butter since it's intended to be the filling in a sandwich cookie. It can be made with a more spreadable consistency by increasing the amount of almond oil in the recipe by a quarter cup. This butter is featured in Happily Ever After Cookies (page 186).

5¾ cups (28.8 ounces) roasted, unsalted almonds

⅔ cup (5.3 ounces) roasted almond oil

¾ teaspoon sea salt

⅔ cup (8 ounces) honey

Place the almonds in the work bowl of a food processor fitted with a steel blade and process for 45 seconds. With the motor running, add the oil in a thin, steady stream through the feed tube. Run the food processor for 1½ minutes, inclusive of the amount of time it takes to add the oil. Add the honey and pulse just to incorporate. (You will see that the honey causes the almond butter to firm up. The longer you take to incorporate the honey, the stiffer the almond butter will get, so don't overdo it.)

Store the nut butter in covered glass jars or plastic containers in the refrigerator for up to one month. Bring to room temperature before using.

NUTTY-ELLA
(Chocolate Hazelnut Spread)

MAKES ABOUT 4 CUPS

While roasted hazelnuts are often what you find at the supermarket, this recipe will turn out even tastier if you roast your own. And your house will smell marvelous while you're doing it. This spread is featured in the Doris Seymour sundae (page 115) and the Sweet Daddy Cookies (page 187).

5 cups (25 ounces) roasted, unsalted hazelnuts or raw hazelnuts

⅔ cup (5.3 ounces) roasted hazelnut oil

1¼ teaspoon vanilla bean paste

¾ teaspoon sea salt

2 cups (8.6 ounces) confectioners' sugar

⅔ cup (2.7 ounces) Dutch-processed cocoa powder

If you're roasting the hazelnuts, preheat the oven to 350°F. Spread the nuts out on a rimmed baking sheet and roast until they're beginning to brown, the skins are splitting, and they smell toasted, about 10 minutes. Shake the pan from time to time so the nuts brown more evenly and don't overbake and become bitter-tasting. Don't bother removing the skins: it's a pain in the neck and not necessary for this recipe. Let the nuts cool to room temperature before proceeding with the recipe.

Place the hazelnuts in the work bowl of a food processor fitted with a steel blade and process for 45 seconds. With the motor running, add the oil in a thin, steady stream through the feed tube. Run the food processor for 1½ minutes, inclusive of the amount of time it takes to add the oil. Add the vanilla paste and salt and pulse a few times to combine.

Sift the confectioners' sugar and cocoa directly into the work bowl of the food processor. Pulse to combine everything, using a rubber spatula, if necessary, to coax the dry ingredients into the nut mixture. Stop pulsing as soon as everything comes together and the spread is a uniform consistency and color.

Store the nut butter in covered glass jars or plastic containers in the refrigerator for up to 1 month. Bring to room temperature before using.

VARIATION

Grilled Nutty-Ella Sandwich Spread ¼ cup Nutty-Ella between 2 pieces of multigrain bread. Melt ½ tablespoon butter in a nonstick pan over medium-low heat and drop in the sandwich, cooking until it's toasted on one side. Melt another ½ tablespoon of butter in the pan, flip the sandwich over, and cook until toasted on the second side. Cut in half and serve immediately.

PEANUT BUTTER

Spanish peanuts are the little red-skinned ones that are often used as a topping in ice cream parlors. We use them in our peanut butter because they have a higher oil content than most other peanuts. Valencia or Virginia peanuts are the ones you are probably most familiar with, the kind you eat by the handful. This spread is featured in the Peanut Butter Shake (page 144), the Peanut Butter Cup sundae (page 129), The Elvis sundae (page 138), and the Mr. Potato Head Sundae (page 133).

2½ cups plus 1 tablespoon (13.3 ounces) oil-roasted, salted Spanish peanuts

2½ cups plus 1 tablespoon (13.3 ounces) oil-roasted, unsalted, blanched Valencia or Virginia peanuts

½ cup plus 1 tablespoon (4.5 ounces) roasted peanut oil

⅓ cup plus 2 tablespoons (5.5 ounces) light honey

Place the peanuts in the work bowl of a food processor fitted with a steel blade and process for 45 seconds. With the motor running, add the oil in a thin, steady stream through the feed tube. Run the food processor for 1½ minutes, inclusive of the amount of time it takes to add the oil. The peanut butter should be fairly runny when the oil has been added, the consistency of runny grits. Add the honey and pulse just to incorporate. (You will see that the honey causes the peanut butter to firm up a little. The longer you take to incorporate the honey, the stiffer the peanut butter will get, so don't overdo it.)

Store the nut butter in covered glass jars or plastic containers in the refrigerator for up to 1 month. Bring to room temperature before using.

CANDIED BACON BITS

There's no way to describe this treat other than sinfully delicious. If the King could put bacon on anything, why can't we put it on ice cream? While the recipe calls for the use of our New Orleans Mead Syrup (page 72), we encourage you to try it with some of our other flavors of syrups like Coffee (page 62), Cola (page 64), Ginger (page 66), or even Pineapple (page 75). The directions for initially cooking the bacon in water might seem strange, but the result will be tender, crisp little bits with a satisfying crunch. These are featured in (of course) The Elvis sundae (page 138).

10 slices (about 10 ounces) bacon

¼ cup plus 2 tablespoons (2.6 ounces) firmly packed light brown sugar

2 tablespoons (1 ounce) New Orleans Mead Syrup (page 72), or ¼ cup (2 ounces) maple syrup

Preheat the oven to 350° F.

Lay the strips of bacon side by side in a 12-inch frying pan and add water to cover by ¼ inch. Cook over medium heat for about 20 minutes. The water will boil away and when you begin to hear the well-known sound of bacon sizzling, remove the pan from the heat.

While the bacon is cooking, combine the brown sugar and syrup in a small bowl, stir with a spoon to combine, and set aside.

Oil a rimmed baking sheet and cover it with aluminum foil, then set a wire cooling rack on top of the foil and, using a pastry brush, oil the foil as well. Lay the partially cooked bacon strips out side by side on the wire rack and, using a spoon, drizzle some of the brown sugar mixture down the center of each strip of bacon. (No need to spread it out. That will happen in the oven of its own accord.)

Bake for 15 minutes, or until the bacon is a uniform medium brown color. Remove to a wire rack and let cool for 10 minutes. Loosen the bacon strips and allow them to continue cooling to room temperature, about another 15 minutes.

Chop the bacon into ¼-inch pieces. The candied bacon may be stored refrigerated, in a covered plastic container, for up to 1 week.

WET WALNUTS

If you live in a maple-syrup–producing region, then by all means buy local maple syrup for this recipe. "Sugar shacks," where maple sap is boiled down to make maple syrup, are often small, family-run endeavors. This topping is featured in the Great Pumpkin sundae (page 121).

4 cups (1 pound) walnuts, coarsely chopped

1 cup (8 ounces) cane sugar

1 cup (8 ounces) water

1 cup (8 ounces) maple syrup

Preheat the oven to 325° F. Spread the walnuts out on a nonstick rimmed baking sheet and toast in the oven for 12 minutes. Set aside.

Combine the sugar and water in a saucepan and bring to a simmer over medium heat, stirring gently from time to time with a rubber spatula, until the sugar has dissolved, about 10 minutes. Take care not to slosh sugar crystals onto the sides of the pan. Remove from the heat when the sugar has dissolved.

Combine all the ingredients and stir well with the rubber spatula.

Store the topping in covered glass jars or plastic containers in the refrigerator for up to 1 month. Bring to room temperature before using.

WHIPPED CREAM

Featured on almost all of our sundaes! Use an electric mixer here—your arm will not survive the ordeal of making this with a whisk or an egg beater. If you can evade exhaustion by passing the bowl from one set of hands to another, then the manual version can be attempted.

2 cups (16 ounces) heavy whipping cream

2 tablespoons (0.5 ounce) confectioners' sugar

½ teaspoon vanilla bean paste

Pour the cream into a large bowl (a metal one, if you have it, which will chill more quickly than other materials) and place the bowl, along with the beaters from the electric mixer, in the refrigerator for 30 minutes.

Using an electric mixer fitted with the chilled beaters, beat the cream on medium until soft peaks form. (To test for soft peaks, dip a spoon in the cream and pull it back out. The action should pull up a small "hill," the point of which will flop over. Picture a dog with floppy ears.) Sift the confectioners' sugar into the bowl, add the vanilla paste, and keep beating until stiff peaks form. (Test the same way you did for soft peaks, but this time picture a dog with ears that stick straight up.) Stop beating immediately (or you risk making butter).

Serve within 2 hours, refrigerating the cream if you're not serving it immediately.

CHAPTER THIRTEEN

BAKED GOODS

Biscuits, pies, and cookies are granted their own spotlight on the marble countertop at Brooklyn Farmacy & Soda Fountain, but truth be told, our baked goods often end up in a sundae, and sometimes even a shake.

See, we like a cookie crumbled over our whipped cream. We like a brownie buried under our fudge. And we really like a pecan bar blended in with a shake. The good news is that while many of these baked treats serve as bedrock for a Farmacy sundae, they also stand solidly on their own.

Our recipes are simple, even for those daunted by baking. So relax! Have fun! We're only making three rules:

Follow ingredient lists to the letter. Unlike building a sundae, baking is not forgiving if you skimp on this or add a little too much of that or substitute willy-nilly.

When you are blending liquid and flour, do it gently and stop as soon as they are combined. The more you mix, the more gluten you release and the less tender the final result. That might be good for yeast-raised breads, but for all the recipes here, it's not.

Finally, use the best ingredients you can. Refer to Resources (page 206) to see where we get our ingredients for Brooklyn Farmacy.

TIPS FOR MEASURING

We have Fannie Farmer to thank for our present system of measurement in the kitchen. She molded chaos into a workable structure when she introduced standardized measuring spoons and cups in her 1896 book *The Boston Cooking-School Cook Book*. Though we are exceedingly grateful for her contribution to cookery, we recommend using a kitchen scale for most of our recipes. (Amazon sells the EatSmart Precision Pro Digital Kitchen Scale for twenty-five dollars.)

We recognize, however, that differentiating between measuring volume and measuring weight can be confounding and frustrating. Generally speaking, all liquid ingredients are measured in volume (pints, quarts, liquid ounces) and all dry ingredients are measured by weight. But some things, like honey, are weighed rather than measured in volume. Phooey, there goes our rule of thumb. To determine whether it should be weighed or put in a measuring cup, look at the label for whatever it is you're using. If the metric measurement is specified in milliliters (ml) or liters (L), then you can use a measuring cup. If the metric measurement is specified in grams (g) or kilograms (kg), then you can bust out your kitchen scale.

BLONDIES

A blondie owes its flavor almost entirely to brown sugar, so use a good one with lots of flavor. We use Billington's Light Brown Muscovado sugar. It can be found in specialty food stores and larger natural food stores. These are featured in the Hey, Blondie! sundae (page 123).

1½ cups (7.5 ounces) all-purpose flour

1 teaspoon baking powder

½ teaspoon baking soda

½ teaspoon sea salt

1¼ cups (8.8 ounces) firmly packed light brown sugar

¾ cup (6 ounces) unsalted butter, browned and cooled to room temperature (see page 157)

1 large egg, at room temperature, slightly beaten

2 teaspoons pure vanilla extract

2 teaspoons dark rum

1 cup (4 ounces) roasted, unsalted almonds, coarsely chopped

Preheat the oven to 350°F.

In a large bowl, combine the flour, baking powder, baking soda, and salt and stir with a fork. Set aside.

Place the brown sugar in a separate bowl and pour the butter over it. Stir with a wooden spoon to combine, breaking up any stubborn lumps of brown sugar in the process. Add the egg and mix thoroughly, then add the vanilla and rum and stir again.

Make a depression in the center of the dry ingredients, pour in the wet ingredients, and fold them in with a rubber spatula, stopping as soon as the ingredients come together. Gently fold in the almonds.

Spread the batter in a nonstick 9 by 13-inch baking pan. (The batter is very stiff, so use your rubber spatula to gently push the batter to the corners of the pan. Don't smash it down, though, or your Blondies will bake up like hockey pucks. It's okay if you can see small spots of the pan through your batter—it will come out of the oven in a solid sheet.)

Bake until the top is set and pale golden brown, about 15 minutes. Do not overbake! Remove to a wire rack and cool completely in the pan. When cool, cut into squares that are roughly 3 inches by 3 inches.

Individually wrap the squares in plastic and store refrigerated for up to 2 days. They may also be stored frozen for up to 3 months. If frozen, allow 1 hour to defrost each Blondie before serving.

BROWNIES

We use 72 percent dark chocolate chips for our brownies. You can use chopped chocolate bars if you have difficulty locating darker chocolate chips. These are featured in the Brownie Sundae (page 128).

1 cup (8 ounces) unsalted butter

1 cup (6 ounces) bittersweet chocolate chips or chopped dark chocolate

4 large eggs, at room temperature

1½ cups (10.5 ounces) firmly packed light brown sugar

1 teaspoon pure vanilla extract

1 cup (5 ounces) all-purpose flour

Preheat the oven to 350°F.

Melt the butter and chocolate chips in a microwave or in the top of a double boiler. (You can fake a double boiler by placing a heatproof bowl over a saucepan of simmering water. If you go this route, make sure you don't get any water in your chocolate mix or it will seize—go stiff—and become unusable.) Set the chocolate mixture aside to cool until slightly above room temperature. Do not allow the mixture to cool to the point that it thickens and becomes difficult to work with.

In a separate bowl, gently whisk the eggs, then add the sugar and vanilla and whisk to combine, taking care to break up any large chunks of brown sugar. Add the egg mixture to the chocolate mixture and whisk to combine. Gently fold the flour into the batter with a rubber spatula just until combined.

Pour the batter into a nonstick 9 by 13-inch baking pan and spread it out evenly with a rubber spatula. Bake until a toothpick inserted in the center of the brownies emerges without any batter clinging to it, about 20 minutes. Do not overbake! Remove to a wire rack and cool completely in the pan. When cool, cut into squares that are roughly 3 inches by 3 inches.

Individually wrap the squares in plastic and store refrigerated for up to 3 days. They may also be stored frozen for up to 3 months. If frozen, allow 1 hour to defrost each Brownie before serving.

PECAN PIE BARS

Pecan Pie Bars were an invention born of serendipity. One beautiful spring day, while strolling the Smorgasburg food market in Williamsburg, Brooklyn, we stumbled across Ben Ackerley's pecan-laden table. He was there as a representative of his father's pecan orchards, Rio Grande Organics. Needless to say, we soon found ourselves in possession of some mighty fine pecans and dreamed up this recipe to highlight them properly.

A food processor will bring this recipe a little closer to effortlessness, though it can be made without one. Look for vanilla bean paste online or in a gourmet or natural food store with a comprehensive herb and spice section. These are featured in the Pecan Pie Bar Shake (page 148).

SHORTBREAD

1½ cups (7.5 ounces) all-purpose flour

½ cup (2.8 ounces) graham flour

⅓ cup plus 1 tablespoon (2.8 ounces) firmly packed light brown sugar

½ teaspoon sea salt

¾ cup (6 ounces) cold unsalted butter, cut in ½-inch cubes

TOPPING

¾ cup (5.3 ounces) firmly packed light brown sugar

⅓ cup (4 ounces) honey

2 tablespoons (1 ounce) heavy cream

1 teaspoon vanilla bean paste

½ cup (4 ounces) unsalted butter, browned (see page 157)

2 cups (8 ounces) pecans, finely chopped

Preheat the oven to 350°F.

To make the shortbread, place the flours, brown sugar, and salt in the work bowl of a food processor fitted with a steel blade. Pulse a few times to combine, then add the cubed butter and pulse until the mixture looks like coarse bread crumbs and clumps when you squeeze a handful of it in your fist. If you don't have a food processor, you can cut the butter into the dry ingredients with a pastry cutter or two knives. Firmly pat the dough into a nonstick 9 by 13-inch baking pan. Bake until golden brown, 15 to 20 minutes. Remove from the oven to a wire rack and let cool slightly.

While the shortbread is baking, prepare the topping. Put the sugar, honey, cream, and vanilla paste in a saucepan, cover with the browned butter, and stir with a rubber spatula to combine. Place the pan over medium heat and bring the contents to a simmer. Cook for 1 minute, then remove from the heat and stir in the pecans.

To assemble the bars, pour the topping over the still-warm shortbread and spread it out evenly with a rubber spatula. Return the pan to the oven and bake until the topping is bubbling, 15 to 20 minutes. Remove from the oven and let cool on a wire rack for 30 minutes. (These are easier to cut while they're still warm.) Cut into bars that are roughly 3 inches by 3 inches.

Individually wrap the bars in plastic and store at room temperature for up to 3 days. They may also be stored frozen for up to 3 months. If frozen, allow 1 hour to defrost each Pecan Pie Bar before serving.

PB&J THUMBPRINT COOKIES

While these cookies can be made with peanut butter from a jar, they are mind-bending when made with our homemade Peanut Butter (page 174). If you're going the jar route, buy a natural peanut butter that doesn't have a bunch of additives in it.

3 cups (15 ounces) all-purpose flour

½ teaspoon baking powder

½ teaspoon baking soda

¼ teaspoon sea salt

1 cup (8 ounces) unsalted butter, at room temperature

1½ cups plus 1 tablespoon (10.9 oz.) firmly packed light brown sugar

1 cup (9 ounces) Peanut Butter (page 174)

2 large eggs, slightly beaten

2 teaspoons pure vanilla extract

½ cup jam of your choice

Preheat the oven to 350°F.

In a large bowl, combine the flour, baking powder, baking soda, and salt and stir with a fork. Set aside.

In the bowl of an electric mixer fitted with the paddle attachment or in a large bowl and using a wooden spoon, cream the butter until smooth; add the sugar and mix thoroughly. Mix in the Peanut Butter and finally, the eggs and vanilla. Add the dry ingredients to the Peanut Butter mixture and mix just to combine. Chill the dough for 20 minutes before baking. (This is not absolutely necessary, but depending on the oil content of the peanut butter you use, your dough might turn out very soft, sticky, and tricky to work with. You can make the call once your dough is made.)

Drop generous tablespoons of dough onto a nonstick baking sheet, about 2 inches apart, and flatten slightly to 2-inch rounds. With your thumb, make a depression in each cookie about ½ inch deep and fill with ½ teaspoon of jam. Bake until the cookie dough is slightly brown and no longer shiny, about 10 minutes. Remove to a wire rack and cool completely.

Store refrigerated for up to 3 days in a covered plastic container, separating layers of cookies with wax paper or parchment. Unbaked cookie dough may be frozen, securely wrapped in plastic wrap, for up to 3 months. Allow frozen dough to soften for 30 minutes in the refrigerator before baking cookies.

OH SNAPS!

While this recipe was developed for use in ice cream sandwiches, it's too good to relegate to that use exclusively. Add a little crystallized ginger and these ascend to a new plane of yumminess. Crystallized ginger may be found in Asian markets or the candy section of larger supermarkets.

Ginger Wafer dough (page 193)

⅓ cup (2 ounces) crystallized ginger, minced

Mix the crystallized ginger into the dough. Form the dough into 2 logs that are each about 1¼ inches in diameter by 10 inches long. Wrap them securely in plastic wrap and freeze until firm enough to slice, about 1 hour.

Preheat the oven to 350°F.

Cut the logs into slices that are 3/16 inch thick. (Try to keep your slices as uniform as possible so that they bake evenly. The first and last cookies from the logs may be a little funny looking, but bake them anyway.) Place the slices 1½ inches apart on nonstick baking sheets. Bake until they are uniformly golden brown, about 10 minutes. Let the cookies cool on the the baking sheets for 3 minutes before removing them to a wire rack to cool completely.

Store in a covered plastic container at room temperature for up to 1 week. Dough logs, wrapped securely in plastic wrap, may be stored frozen for up to 3 months. Allow frozen dough to soften for 30 minutes in the refrigerator before slicing and baking.

HAPPILY EVER AFTER COOKIES

The name for these cookies makes more sense when you know that they were invented for Valentine's Day at Brooklyn Farmacy. At the beginning of February every year, we provide our customers with red construction paper hearts and markers and encourage them to proclaim their love on paper. The valentines are then stuffed into a red "mailbox" set out on our counter. On February 13, we stay up late and string the Valentines in our store windows for the whole world (or our little section of Brooklyn) to see. We felt the need to honor this grand display of love somehow, and so the Happily Ever After was born.

Though our Almond Butter is exceptional in this cookie, they can be assembled with store-bought almond butter. Look for a natural one with a minimum of additives.

Vanilla Wafer dough (page 192)

¾ to 1 cup Almond Butter (page 172)

Form the dough into 2 logs that are each about 1¼ inches in diameter by 10 inches long. Wrap them securely in plastic wrap and freeze until firm enough to slice, about 1 hour.

Preheat the oven to 350°F.

Cut the logs into slices that are ¼ inch thick. (Try to keep your slices as uniform as possible so that they bake evenly. The first and last cookies from the logs may be a little funny looking, but bake them anyway.) Place the slices 1½ inches apart on nonstick baking sheets. Bake until the edges of the cookies are beginning to brown and the tops are no longer shiny, 5 to 6 minutes. Let the cookies cool on the baking sheets for 3 minutes before removing them to a wire rack to cool completely.

When the cookies are cool, sandwich about 1 teaspoon of Almond Butter between 2 cookies and, with the cookie on a flat surface, gently press on it to squeeze the filling to the edges of the cookie.

Store in a covered plastic container at room temperature for up to 3 days. Dough logs, wrapped securely in plastic wrap, may be stored frozen for up to 3 months. Allow frozen dough to soften for 30 minutes in the refrigerator before slicing and baking.

SWEET DADDY COOKIES

MAKES ABOUT 2 DOZEN COOKIES

This cookie dough, a hazelnut shortbread, can be made most easily in a food processor. The dough can also be made by hand if you don't have a food processor. Refer to the recipe for Nutty-Ella (page 173) if you're toasting raw hazelnuts. If you're not making our Nutty-Ella, substitute a good quality chocolate hazelnut spread.

1½ cups (7.5 ounces) all-purpose flour

1 cup (8 ounces) cold unsalted butter, cut in ½-inch cubes

½ cup (2.2 ounces) confectioners' sugar

½ cup (2.5 ounces) roasted, unsalted hazelnuts, ground

¼ teaspoon sea salt

½ cup Nutty-Ella (page 173)

Put the flour and butter in the work bowl of a food processor fitted with a steel blade and pulse until the mixture looks like coarse bread crumbs and clumps when you squeeze a handful of it in your fist. (If you don't have a food processor, you can cut the butter into the flour with a pastry cutter or two knives.) Add the sugar, hazelnuts, and salt and pulse to combine thoroughly (or cut them into the flour and butter mixture by hand).

Form the dough into 2 logs that are each about 1¼ inches in diameter by 11 inches long. Wrap them securely in plastic wrap and freeze until firm enough to slice, about 1 hour.

Preheat the oven to 375°F.

Cut the logs in slices that are ¼ inch thick. (Try to keep your slices as uniform as possible so that they bake evenly. The first and last cookies from the logs may be a little funny looking, but bake them anyway.) Place the slices 1½ inches apart on nonstick baking sheets. Bake until the edges of the cookies are beginning to brown, about 11 minutes. Let the cookies cool on the cookie sheets for 3 minutes before removing them to a wire rack to cool completely.

When the cookies are cool, sandwich about 1 teaspoon of Nutty-Ella between 2 cookies and, with the cookie on a flat surface, gently press on it to squeeze the filling to the edges of the cookie.

Store in a covered plastic container at room temperature for up to 3 days. Dough logs, wrapped securely in plastic wrap, may be stored frozen for up to 3 months. Allow frozen dough to soften for 30 minutes in the refrigerator before slicing and baking.

CHOCOLATE WHOOPIE CAKES

The best part about a birthday cake (if you're not a cuckoo-for-frosting kind of person) is the way it sops up melty ice cream to make a heavenly tasting mush. When we started serving Chocolate Whoopie Pies (opposite) at the Farmacy, it seemed like a natural leap to incorporate these little cakes into a sundae. While the batter is easy enough to put together, the cakes are persnickety when it comes to baking. Pay close attention to the baking instructions. You want the cakes to be baked through so they don't collapse in the center, but not dry, which happens if you overbake them. These cakes are featured in the Makin' Whoopie! Sundae (page 126) and the Chocolate Whoopie Pie (opposite).

1⅔ cups (8.4 ounces) all-purpose flour

⅔ cup (2.7 ounces) Dutch-processed cocoa powder

1½ teaspoons baking soda

½ teaspoon sea salt

½ cup (4 ounces) unsalted butter, at room temperature

1 cup plus 3 tablespoons (8.3 ounces) firmly packed light brown sugar

2 large eggs, at room temperature

1 teaspoon pure vanilla extract

1 cup (8 ounces) buttermilk

Position one oven rack in the upper third position in your oven and a second rack in the lower third position. Line two baking sheets with parchment paper or silicone mats. Preheat the oven to 350°F.

Combine the flour, cocoa, baking soda, and salt in a bowl. Set aside.

In the bowl of an electric mixer fitted with the paddle attachment or in a large bowl and using a wooden spoon, cream the butter until smooth; add the sugar and mix thoroughly. Add the eggs, one at a time, stirring well after each addition. Stir in the vanilla. Add half of the flour mixture and half of the buttermilk to the batter and fold it in with a rubber spatula, mixing just until incorporated. Add the remaining flour mixture and buttermilk, again mixing just until incorporated. (You don't want to overmix the batter, but you do need to make sure that the ingredients are thoroughly combined. Isolated lumps of butter or brown sugar will bubble up in the oven and make your cakes look like little volcanoes.)

Drop scant ¼ cups of batter in round mounds spaced 2 inches apart onto the prepared baking sheets. Take care to make the mounds of batter as uniform as possible so they all bake evenly. You should be able to fit 12 to a cookie sheet.

Bake the cakes for 8 minutes and then, quickly and carefully, switch the positions of the cookie sheets in the oven and rotate each sheet 180 degrees. Bake until the center of a cake springs back when you poke it with your finger, another 5 to 6 minutes. (As pictured at right.) Test a few cakes before removing all of them from the oven. Remove to a wire rack and let cool completely.

Store refrigerated in a covered plastic container for up to 2 days. The cakes may be stored frozen, in a covered plastic container, for up to 3 months. Allow 30 minutes to defrost each frozen cake before using.

CHOCOLATE WHOOPIE PIES

MAKES 12 WHOOPIE PIES

The whoopie pie is associated with both the Pennsylvania Amish and New England as a whole. It is in fact, the official state "treat" of Maine. Although the whoopie filling makes more than you'll need to assemble twelve Whoopie Pies, it will keep in the refrigerator in a covered plastic container for up to three weeks. It can be used for other purposes as well, like frosting cupcakes.

½ cup (4 ounces) unsalted butter, at room temperature

1 (8-ounce) package cream cheese, at room temperature

3 cups (12.9 ounces) confectioners' sugar

1 teaspoon vanilla bean paste

Chocolate Whoopie Cakes (opposite), baked and cooled

In the bowl of an electric mixer fitted with the paddle attachment or in a bowl and using a wooden spoon, cream the butter and cream cheese until smooth; add the sugar and mix thoroughly. Stir in the vanilla. Chill before using.

To assemble the pies, lay one half of the cakes, flat-side up, on a work surface. Fill a pastry bag with the whoopie filling and pipe 2 to 3 tablespoons in a circle onto each cake, leaving a ½-inch border between the outer edge of the filling and the edge of the cake. (You can make a pastry bag by snipping a corner from a resealable plastic bag. Put the filling in the bag first though!) Put a second cake, flat side down, on top and press gently on it to squeeze the filling to the edges of the cake, then serve immediately.

Assembled Whoopie Pies may be kept refrigerated in a covered plastic container for up to 1 day. Bring to room temperature before serving. The Whoopie Pie filling will keep refrigerated in a covered plastic container for up to 2 weeks.

CHOCOLATE WAFERS

MAKES ABOUT 2 DOZEN COOKIES

This is a fudgy cookie, strong enough to stand up to a scoop of ice cream, yet with some give to it, so it yields pleasingly when you bite into it. The better the cocoa powder used in this recipe, the better the wafers will taste. This cookie is featured in the Ice Cream Sandwich (page 194).

2¼ cups (11.3 ounces) all-purpose flour

1 cup plus 2 tablespoons (4.5 ounces) Dutch-processed cocoa powder

1¾ cups plus 2 tablespoons (13.1 ounces) firmly packed light brown sugar

½ teaspoon sea salt

1⅓ cups (10.6 ounces) cold unsalted butter, cut in ½-inch cubes

¼ cup plus 1 tablespoon (2.5 ounces) whole milk

1½ teaspoons pure vanilla extract

Combine the flour, cocoa, sugar, and salt in the bowl of a food processor fitted with a steel blade. Process for 10 seconds to combine. Add the butter and pulse 30 times, for 1 second each time. (If you don't have a food processor, you can cut the butter into the dry ingredients with a pastry cutter or two knives, stopping when the mixture looks like coarse bread crumbs and clumps when you squeeze a handful of it in your fist.) Combine the milk and vanilla and, with the motor running, add to the dough through the feed tube. Hit the stop button when the dough comes together into a solid mass. (If you're making the dough by hand, add the liquid ingredients to the dry ingredients and stir with a fork. Turn the dough out onto a clean work surface and, with the heel of your hand, push clumps of it away from you to incorporate the butter into the dough more thoroughly. Stop when the dough coheres in a solid mass.)

Form the dough into a log that is about 2½ inches in diameter by 11 inches long. Enclose the log completely in plastic wrap and freeze until firm enough to slice, about 2 hours.

Preheat the oven to 350°F.

Cut the log into slices that are ½ inch thick. (Try to keep your slices as uniform as possible so that they bake evenly. The first and last wafer from the log may be a little funny looking, but bake them anyway.) Place the slices 2 inches apart on nonstick baking sheets. Bake until the tops of the wafers are no longer shiny, about 12 minutes. Let the wafers cool on the cookie sheets for 5 minutes before removing them to a wire rack to cool completely.

Store in a covered plastic container at room temperature for up to 2 days. Dough logs, wrapped securely in plastic wrap, may be stored frozen for up to 3 months. Allow frozen dough to soften for 30 minutes in the refrigerator before slicing and baking. Baked wafers may be stored frozen for up to 3 months in covered plastic containers. Allow 20 minutes to defrost each frozen wafer before using. If you are using the wafers for ice cream sandwiches, there is no need to defrost them.

VANILLA WAFERS

A chocolate ice cream sandwich wafer would be lonely without a vanilla counterpart. These wafers have a rich butterscotch flavor, especially if you use a great-tasting brown sugar, and are wonderful with ice cream flavors like toffee, butter almond, pecan, or salted caramel. They can even hold their own when they enclose a scoop of chocolate ice cream. This cookie is featured in the Ice Cream Sandwich (page 194) and the Happily Ever After Cookies (page 186).

2 cups (10 ounces) all-purpose flour

½ teaspoon baking powder

½ teaspoon baking soda

1 teaspoon sea salt

1 cup (8 ounces) unsalted butter, at room temperature

½ cup (4 ounces) cane sugar

¾ cup (5.3 ounces) firmly packed light brown sugar

2 large egg yolks

2 tablespoons vanilla bean paste

In a large bowl, combine the flour, baking powder, baking soda, and salt and stir with a fork. Set aside.

In the bowl of an electric mixer fitted with the paddle attachment or in a large bowl and using a wooden spoon, cream the butter until smooth; add the sugars and mix thoroughly. Add the egg yolks, one at a time, stirring well after each addition. Mix in the vanilla paste. Add the dry ingredients to the butter mixture and mix just to combine.

Form the dough into a log that is about 2½ inches in diameter by 10 inches long. Enclose the log completely in plastic wrap and freeze until firm enough to slice, about 2 hours.

Preheat the oven to 350°F.

Cut the log into slices that are ⅜ inch thick. (Try to keep your slices as uniform as possible so that they bake evenly. The first and last wafer from the log may be a little funny looking, but bake them anyway.) Place the slices 2 inches apart on nonstick baking sheets. Bake until the edges of the wafers are beginning to brown and the tops are no longer shiny, 7 to 9 minutes. Let the wafers cool on the cookie sheets for 5 minutes before removing them to a wire rack to cool completely.

Store in a covered plastic container at room temperature for up to 2 days. Dough logs, wrapped securely in plastic wrap, may be stored frozen for up to 3 months. Allow frozen dough to soften for 30 minutes in the refrigerator before slicing and baking. Baked wafers may be stored frozen for up to 3 months in covered plastic containers. Allow 20 minutes to defrost each frozen wafer before using. If you are using the wafers for ice cream sandwiches, there is no need to defrost them.

GINGER WAFERS

Cane syrup is not easy to find, but it's well worth seeking out. It definitely tastes like a relative to molasses, but its flavor is cleaner and more vibrant. In Abbeville, Louisiana, five generations of Steens have produced cane syrup since the C. S. Steen's Syrup Mill opened in 1910. Cane syrup mills were once abundant in the South, but Steen's is now one of the few that remain. If you can't find true cane syrup, you can substitute Lyle's Golden Syrup, an English product that has recently become easier to find in the States in well-stocked markets. And if you can't find Lyle's Golden Syrup, then use a good-quality molasses. These cookies are featured in the Ice Cream Sandwich (page 194) and the Oh Snaps! cookies (page 185).

2 cups (10 ounces) all-purpose flour

1 teaspoon baking soda

¼ teaspoon sea salt

2 teaspoons ground cinnamon

1½ teaspoons ground ginger

¼ teaspoon ground allspice

⅛ teaspoon ground cloves

⅛ teaspoon freshly ground black pepper

10 tablespoons (5 ounces) unsalted butter, at room temperature

⅔ cup (5.4 ounces) cane sugar

1 large egg yolk

½ teaspoon pure vanilla extract

¼ cup (2 ounces) cane syrup or molasses

In a large bowl, combine the flour, baking soda, salt, cinnamon, ginger, allspice, cloves, and pepper and stir with a fork. Set aside.

In the bowl of an electric mixer fitted with the paddle attachment or in another large bowl and using a wooden spoon, cream the butter until smooth; add the sugar and mix thoroughly. Add the egg yolk and stir well. Mix in the vanilla and cane syrup.

Add the dry ingredients to the butter mixture and mix just to combine. Form the dough into a log that is about 2½ inches in diameter by 9 inches long. Enclose the log completely in plastic wrap and freeze until firm enough to slice, about 2 hours.

Preheat the oven to 350°F.

Cut the log into slices that are ⅜ inch thick. (Try to keep your slices as uniform as possible so that they bake evenly. The first and last wafer from the log may be a little funny looking, but bake them anyway.) Place the slices about 2 inches apart on nonstick baking sheets. Bake for 12 minutes. Let the wafers cool on the cookie sheets for 5 minutes before removing them to a wire rack to cool completely.

Store in a covered plastic container at room temperature for up to 2 days. Dough logs, wrapped securely in plastic wrap, may be stored frozen for up to 3 months. Allow frozen dough to soften for 30 minutes in the refrigerator before slicing and baking. Baked wafers may be stored frozen for up to 3 months in covered plastic containers. Allow 20 minutes to defrost each frozen wafer before using. If you are using the wafers for ice cream sandwiches, there is no need to defrost them.

ICE CREAM SANDWICH

A 1901 column in the *New York Mail* said: "As a new fad, the ice-cream sandwich might have made thousands of dollars for its inventor had the novelty been launched by a well-known caterer, but strangely enough the ice-cream sandwich made its advent in a humble Bowery pushcart." A handful of references to the ice cream sandwich from the early 1900s can be found, though none are specific about who invented this quintessentially American treat. What is known is that they were considered the treat for the "common folk" and were originally hawked by street vendors.

While ice cream sandwiches have gone through many incarnations, like the It's It and the Chipwich, at the fountain we serve up a straightforward sandwich that can be enjoyed with a variety of wafer and ice cream flavors. These are an ideal dessert to make in advance of a birthday party or special event. Easy to make and delightful to serve, your guests will be charmed when you present these at the end of a meal.

2 Chocolate (page 190), Vanilla (page 192), or Ginger (page 193) Wafers

1 (4-ounce) scoop ice cream, any flavor

Before starting, make sure your ice cream is not rock hard. Let it soften on your countertop for 10 minutes or microwave it on high for 5 seconds. To make an ice cream sandwich, place a 4-ounce scoop of ice cream between 2 wafers and, with the bottom cookie on a flat surface, gently press on the top cookie with the flat of your hand to squeeze the ice cream to the edges of the wafers. Let harden in the freezer for at least 2 hours before serving.

VARIATIONS

Follow the directions for making an Ice Cream Sandwich but spread 1 tablespoon Peanut Butter (page 174), Nutty-Ella (page 173), Hot Fudge (page 161), or Caramel Sauce (page 162) on the inside of the top cookie before placing it on the scoop of ice cream.

VANILLA CAKES

These very versatile cakes can be utilized in a number of ways. Try them with vanilla ice cream and Blackberry Compote (page 167), Blueberry Compote (page 166), Raspberry Compote (page 165), or Strawberry Compote (page 168). Whoa! They are featured in the Affugazi Affogato sundae (page 112).

2½ cups (12.5 ounces) all-purpose flour

2 teaspoons baking powder

¼ teaspoon baking soda

1 teaspoon sea salt

1 cup (8 ounces) unsalted butter, at room temperature

1¾ cups (14 ounces) cane sugar

3 large eggs, at room temperature

1 teaspoon pure vanilla extract

¾ cup (6 ounces) buttermilk

Preheat the oven to 350°F. Line a standard muffin tin with paper liners.

Combine the flour, baking powder, baking soda, and salt in a bowl. Set aside.

In the bowl of an electric mixer fitted with the paddle attachment or in a bowl and using a wooden spoon, cream the butter until smooth; add the sugar and mix thoroughly. Add the eggs, one at a time, stirring well after each addition. Stir in the vanilla. Add one-third of the flour mixture to the batter and fold it in with a rubber spatula, mixing just until incorporated. Then add half of the buttermilk, again mixing just until incorporated. Add another one-third of the flour, then the remaining buttermilk, and finally the remaining flour, taking care not to overmix the batter.

Drop dollops of the batter into the muffin cups, filling each muffin cup about three-fourths full. Bake until the cupcakes are golden brown and spring back when you poke them gently in the center with your finger, about 20 minutes. Remove to a wire rack and allow to cool in the muffin tin for 10 minutes. Invert the cakes onto a wire rack and allow to cool completely before serving.

The cakes may be stored, securely wrapped in plastic wrap, in the refrigerator for up to 2 days. Allow to come to room temperature before serving. The cakes may be frozen, individually wrapped in plastic wrap, for up to 3 months. Allow 1 hour to defrost each cake before serving.

SPICE BUNDT CAKE

Although this cake has a lot of ingredients with bold flavors, its overall flavor is actually very well-balanced. In order for it to turn out that way though, you'll need to use a darker honey (wildflower is really nice and widely available, or buckwheat), brew your coffee strong, and use a good-quality dark rum (try Myers's, Gosling's Black Seal, or The Kraken Black Spiced Rum). One medium orange should yield you ⅓ cup of juice; use 2 oranges if they're small or particularly dry. This cake is featured in the Spice Cake Sundae (page 120). We specify baking this cake in a 9-inch springform Bundt pan; it can certainly be made in a traditional Bundt pan, but the springform version will banish any anxiety you might have about whether or not your cake will release from the pan once it's baked.

2⅓ cups (11.7 ounces) all-purpose flour

¾ teaspoon baking powder

¾ teaspoon baking soda

½ teaspoon sea salt

2½ teaspoons cinnamon

½ teaspoon allspice

¼ teaspoon ground cloves

1 cup (8 ounces) cane sugar

¼ cup (1.8 ounces) firmly packed light brown sugar

⅔ cup (5.4 ounces) canola oil

⅔ cup (8 ounces) honey

⅔ cup (5.4 ounces) freshly brewed strong coffee, warm

⅓ cup (2.6 ounces) freshly squeezed orange juice

3 tablespoons (1.5 ounces) dark rum

2 large eggs, at room temperature, slightly beaten

¾ teaspoon pure vanilla extract

Preheat the oven to 350° F. Butter and flour a 9-inch springform Bundt pan.

In a large bowl, combine the flour, baking powder, baking soda, salt, and spices and whisk to combine.

In a separate medium bowl, combine the sugars and break up any lumps in the brown sugar with your fingers. Add the canola oil, honey, coffee, orange juice, rum, eggs, and vanilla, one at a time, stirring well with a wooden spoon after each addition to combine.

Make a depression in the center of the dry ingredients and pour in the wet ingredients. Fold them together with a rubber spatula, mixing just until incorporated.

Pour the batter into the prepared Bundt pan. Bake for 50 minutes, or until a skewer inserted into the center of the cake emerges clean. Remove the cake from the oven and let cool for 15 minutes on a wire rack. Run a paring knife between the cake and the exterior springform band, then pop the latch to release the band and lift it straight up to remove it. Place a plate upside-down over the pan, and, holding on tightly, invert both to release the cake. If the cake doesn't release in a few seconds, you might need to gently loosen it by running your paring knife between the cake and the pan, taking care not to cut into your cake. Let the cake cool completely on the wire rack before serving.

The cake may be stored, securely wrapped in plastic wrap, in the refrigerator for up to 3 days. Allow to come to room temperature before serving. The cake may also be frozen, securely wrapped in plastic wrap, for up to 3 months. Allow 2 hours to defrost before serving.

PIE CRUST

This pie dough is a snap to make in a food processor, but it can be made by hand, too. It will keep, bundled up in plastic wrap, in the freezer for up to 3 months, so you may as well make extra while you're at it. The crust is featured in the Pie Crust Crumble (page 152) and all our pies!

2¼ cups (11.3 ounces) all-purpose flour

1 cup plus 2 tablespoons (4.5 ounces) cake flour

3 tablespoons (1.5 ounces) cane sugar

½ teaspoon sea salt

1½ cups (12 ounces) cold unsalted butter, cut in ½-inch cubes

¾ cup (6 ounces) ice water

Place the flours, sugar, and salt in the work bowl of a food processor fitted with a steel blade. Pulse a few times to combine, then add 1 cup of the butter and pulse 5 or 6 times to reduce the butter to pea-size pieces. Add the remaining ½ cup butter and, with the motor running, pour the water in through the feed tube. Pulse 2 or 3 times, until the dough comes together. (If you don't have a food processor, you can cut the butter into the dry ingredients with a pastry cutter or two knives.) The dough should look like ground cornmeal with a smattering of peas in it and will hold together in a mass when you press a handful of it together. Add water by droplets if the dough is too dry and stop as soon as it coheres. (It's important not to add too much water to the dough, or it will be tough when you bake it. And work rapidly so your butter doesn't have a chance to melt. It's okay if there are small lumps of butter in the mixture when you're done.)

Empty the dough onto a large, rectangular piece of plastic wrap and separate it into 2 equal-size mounds. Pat the mounds into chunky pancakes about 8 inches in diameter. Cut the plastic wrap in half and wrap up each crust individually. Let the crusts rest in the freezer for at least 2 hours before using.

Unbaked pie crust may be frozen, securely wrapped in plastic wrap, for up to 3 months. Thaw in the refrigerator overnight before using.

BLUEBERRY PIE

Quick-cooking tapioca (derived from the root of the tropical cassava plant) is brilliant for thickening fruit fillings in pies and can easily be found in the baking section of most supermarkets. Not only does it mean that you will no longer have fruit soup floating in the bottom of your pie plate, but its flavor is undetectable and it imparts a pleasing glossy sheen to your fruit filling. Be certain to let the filling sit for at least five minutes once you've combined the fruit and tapioca. This will ensure that the tapioca absorbs liquid from the fruit when you bake the pie. You must also let the pie cool (completely!) before serving in order for the tapioca to set properly. Forewarned is forearmed: cooling takes about 4 hours.

Pie Crust (opposite), separated into two lumps of dough

3 pints fresh blueberries, or 36 ounces frozen blueberries

1 tablespoon freshly squeezed lemon juice

1 teaspoon freshly grated lemon zest

1 cup (8 ounces) cane sugar

6 tablespoons (2.2 ounces) quick-cooking tapioca

¼ teaspoon sea salt

⅛ teaspoon dried lavender flowers

1 tablespoon (0.5 ounce) unsalted butter, cut into bits

Egg wash: 1 large egg, slightly beaten with 1 tablespoon (0.5 ounce) water

Line a baking sheet with parchment paper or a silicone mat.

For the crust, on a lightly floured surface, roll out 1 lump of the crust dough to a 13-inch round, working quickly so the dough remains cold. Place it in a 9-inch deep-dish pie plate and let the edges of the crust drape over the side of the plate. Roll out the remaining lump of crust dough to a 10-inch round and place it on the prepared baking sheet. This will be your top crust. Let both rest in the freezer while the pie filling is assembled.

Preheat the oven to 400°F.

To make the filling, in a large bowl, combine the blueberries, lemon juice and zest, sugar, tapioca, salt, and lavender. Mix thoroughly and let sit at room temperature for 10 minutes.

Put the filling in the chilled bottom crust and dot with the butter bits. Brush the edges of the lower crust with egg wash and lay the top crust over the berries. Crimp the edges of the crusts with a fork to seal them together, then brush the top of the pie with the egg wash. Cut vent holes in the top crust. (You may also top the pie with a lattice crust if you're so inclined.) Let the pie rest in the freezer for 15 minutes before baking.

Bake for 20 minutes. Decrease the oven temperature to 350°F and continue to bake until the crust is golden brown and the filling is bubbling, 25 to 30 minutes. Remove from the oven and let cool completely on a wire rack before serving, about 4 hours.

The pie may be refrigerated, securely wrapped in plastic wrap, for up to 2 days. Allow to come to room temperature before serving.

APPLE CRUMB PIE

There's nothing quite like a homemade apple pie. It may take a bit of effort, but the rewards are immeasurable. This recipe may be made with a double crust if you prefer that over the Crumb Topping (make the full crust recipe). Use an assortment of apple varieties—any kinds, really—which will give your pie a broader spectrum of flavors and better texture.

CRUMB TOPPING

¾ cup (3.8 ounces) all-purpose flour

¾ cup (2.8 ounces) rolled oats

½ cup plus 2 tablespoons (4.4 ounces) firmly packed light brown sugar

¾ teaspoon sea salt

¾ cup (6 ounces) cold unsalted butter, cut in ½-inch cubes

½ recipe Pie Crust (page 198)

APPLE FILLING

5 medium to large apples (about 2 pounds), peeled, quartered, and cored

1 tablespoon freshly squeezed lemon juice

½ cup (4 ounces) cane sugar

3 tablespoons (1.3 ounces) firmly packed light brown sugar

1 teaspoon ground cinnamon

4 tablespoons (2 ounces) unsalted butter

3 tablespoons (0.9 ounce) all-purpose flour

2 tablespoons (1 ounce) water

To make the topping, combine all the ingredients in a bowl. Working nimbly and quickly so your butter doesn't melt, incorporate the butter into the dry ingredients by rubbing them together with your fingertips. You can break up larger lumps of butter by squeezing them between your fingertips. When the mixture darkens and looks moist, you're done. Refrigerate the mixture until ready to use.

For the crust, on a lightly floured surface, roll out the crust to a 13-inch round, working quickly so the dough remains cold. Set the dough in a 9-inch deep dish pie plate, fold under any excess dough that might be hanging over the edge of the pie plate, and use a fork to crimp the edges of the crust. Let the crust rest in the freezer while the pie filling is assembled.

Preheat the oven to 375°F.

To make the filling, cut the apples in thin lengthwise slices (no thicker than ¼ inch). You should wind up with about 7 cups of sliced apples. Toss the apples in a large bowl with the lemon juice and set aside.

In a small bowl, combine the cane and brown sugars and cinnamon. Set aside. Melt the butter in a small saucepan. Remove it from the heat and stir in the flour. Stir in the sugar mixture, then the 2 tablespoons water.

To bake the pie, place the apple filling in the chilled crust and top with the sugar mixture, avoiding the exposed edges of the pie crust. Bake for 25 minutes. Remove the pie from the oven, sprinkle on the topping, and return it to the oven. Decrease the oven temperature to 350°F and bake until the crust and topping are golden brown and a toothpick inserted in the pie encounters no resistance (which indicates that your apples are cooked through), about 35 minutes more. Remove from the oven and let cool on a wire rack for at least 1 hour before serving.

The pie may be refrigerated, securely wrapped in plastic wrap, for up to 2 days. Allow to come to room temperature before serving.

PECAN PIE

Pecan pie can have that cloying sweetness to it that makes you feel like booking an appointment with your dentist right after eating a slice. This version, which contains no corn syrup, is just right. Make sure your pecans are fresh since they have the spotlight in this recipe. (Pictured on page 202.)

½ recipe Pie Crust (page 198)

3 large eggs

¾ cup (6 ounces) unsalted butter, melted

1 cup plus 3 tablespoons (8.3 ounces) firmly packed light brown sugar

¼ cup plus 2 tablespoons (3 ounces) cane sugar

4½ teaspoons (0.5 ounce) all-purpose flour

4½ teaspoons (0.5 ounce) whole milk

1½ teaspoons pure vanilla extract

1½ cups (6 ounces) pecan halves, coarsely chopped

Whole pecans for decoration

On a lightly floured surface, roll out the crust to a 13-inch round, working quickly so the dough remains cold. Place it in a 9-inch deep-dish pie plate, fold under any excess dough that might be hanging over the edge of the pie plate, and use a fork to crimp the edges of the crust. Let it rest in the freezer for 20 minutes.

Preheat the oven to 400°F.

Prebake the pie crust: Line the chilled crust with parchment paper or aluminum foil and fill it with pie weights (see Resources, page 206). Bake it for 10 minutes, remove it from the oven, and gently remove the weights by gathering up the corners of the paper or foil to make a bundle, and lifting straight up. Return the crust to the oven until the center of the crust is no longer shiny and moist-looking, 5 to 10 minutes. Remove the crust to a wire rack to cool while you assemble the filling.

In a medium bowl, whisk the eggs until foamy, then whisk in the melted butter. Stir in the sugars and flour and mix thoroughly. Stir in the milk and vanilla and then the pecans. Pour the mixture into the prebaked pie crust. Decorate the top of the pie with whole pecans. (Just let them float on the top of the filling and take care not to jostle the pie as you put it in the oven or you will wreck your pretty design.)

Bake for 10 minutes. Then decrease the oven temperature to 350°F and bake until the crust is golden brown and the filling no longer jiggles when you shake the pie, 25 to 35 minutes. (If the center is vaguely jiggly, that's perfect. The pie will be dry if you bake it until the center is completely stiff.) Remove it from the oven and let cool completely on a wire rack before serving, about 4 hours.

The pie may be refrigerated, securely wrapped in plastic wrap, for up to 2 days. Allow to come to room temperature before serving.

PUMPKIN PIE

The best pumpkins for making pumpkin pie are the broad, squat ones that look like someone sat on them, to be specific *Cucurbita moschata*. The best place to find these is at a farmers' market or health food store during fall apple season (usually October in the Northeast). Some varieties to look for are Long Island Cheese and Musquee de Provence. Be sure you buy one that will fit in your oven—these babies grow big!

To roast a whole pumpkin, scoop out the seeds and place the inverted pumpkin on a rimmed baking sheet lined with parchment paper. Bake in a preheated 325°F oven until tender, 1 to 1½ hours. It's done when a skewer inserted into the flesh meets no resistance. When the pumpkin has cooled enough to handle, scoop out the flesh and use a food processor or blender to puree the flesh in manageable batches.

½ recipe Pie Crust
(page 198)

2 cups roasted and pureed pumpkin, or 1 (15-ounce) can pumpkin puree

1 (14-ounce) can sweetened condensed milk

¼ cup (2 ounces) sour cream

2 teaspoons ground cinnamon

1 teaspoon ground ginger

½ teaspoon ground allspice

¼ teaspoon ground cloves

2 large eggs, slightly beaten

½ teaspoon pure vanilla extract

On a lightly floured suface, roll out the crust to a 13-inch round, working quickly so the dough remains cold. Place it in a 9-inch deep-dish pie plate, fold under any excess dough that might be hanging over the edge, and use a fork to crimp the edges of the crust. Let it rest in the freezer for 20 minutes.

Preheat the oven to 400°F.

Prebake the pie crust: Line the frozen crust with parchment paper or aluminum foil and fill it with pie weights (see Resources, page 206). Bake it for 10 minutes, remove it from the oven, and gently remove the weights by gathering up the corners of the paper or foil to make a bundle, and lifting straight up. Return the crust to the oven until the center of the crust is no longer shiny and moist-looking, 5 to 10 minutes. Remove the crust to a wire rack to cool while you assemble the filling. Decrease the oven temperature to 350°F.

In a bowl, combine the pumpkin, sweetened condensed milk, sour cream, cinnamon, ginger, allspice, and cloves and mix thoroughly. In a separate small bowl, combine the eggs and vanilla and pour them into the pumpkin mixture, blending well. Pour the mixture into the prebaked crust. Bake until the crust is golden brown and the filling is puffed around the edges of the crust and jiggles only slightly in the center, about 35 minutes. Allow to cool completely on a wire rack before serving, about 4 hours.

The pie may be refrigerated, securely wrapped in plastic wrap, for up to 2 days. Allow to come to room temperature before serving.

SOUTHERN STYLE
BUTTERMILK BISCUITS

These are darn good for breakfast with butter and preserves. Or try them in berry shortcake with our Blackberry Compote (page 167), Blueberry Compote (page 166), Raspberry Compote (page 165), or Strawberry Compote (page 168). There's a reason certain recipes are handed down from one generation to the next by showing rather than telling. This is one of those recipes that's easier to put across visually than verbally. Be patient and read the recipe directions and you won't be led astray.

4 cups (20 ounces) all-purpose flour

2 tablespoons baking powder

½ teaspoon baking soda

2 teaspoons sea salt

¾ cup (6 ounces) cold unsalted butter, cut in ½-inch cubes

2 cups (16 ounces) buttermilk

Preheat the oven to 450°F. Line a baking sheet with parchment paper or silicone mat.

Combine the flour, baking powder, baking soda, and salt in a large bowl and stir with a fork. Cut the butter into the dry ingredients with a pastry cutter or two knives until the mixture is the texture of coarsely ground cornmeal with a smattering of peas in it. (You want to do this quickly so your butter doesn't melt. It's okay if there are small lumps of butter in the mixture when you're done.)

Make a depression in the center of the dry ingredients and pour the buttermilk into it. Stir with a fork, reaching to the bottom of the bowl, and mix gently just until the ingredients are combined. (Don't overdo it.)

Turn the dough out onto a lightly floured work surface and pat the mixture into a square that is ½ to ¾ inch thick. Fold the dough in half toward you and then rotate it 90 degrees to the right. Keeping the surface lightly floured, flip the dough over toward you and pat down, once again, to a thickness of ½ to ¾ inch. Continue folding, turning, flipping, and patting the dough down, stopping when you've completed a total of 5 cycles. Using a 3-inch square biscuit cutter, you should be able to cut 10 biscuits. Scraps of biscuit dough may be recombined to form complete biscuits, but will have a slightly different texture than the first biscuits cut.

Place the biscuits on the prepared baking sheet, spaced 2 inches apart. Bake until the biscuits are golden brown and have "popped," about 13 minutes. Remove the biscuits to a wire rack to cool. Serve immediately.

Unbaked biscuits may be stored frozen for up to 3 months. To freeze, lay the biscuits out in a single layer on a baking sheet and freeze. Once frozen, transfer them to a covered plastic container. Bake frozen biscuits without defrosting, but allow about 5 minutes more baking time.

RESOURCES

INGREDIENT SOURCES

Adirondack Creamery
www.adirondackcreamery.com
Ice cream used at Farmacy
(and yes, they ship!)

Amazon
www.amazon.com
Assorted ingredients, including
hard-to-find dried hibiscus flowers,
li hing mui powder

American Almond Products Co.
www.americanalmond.com/
    products
Pistachio paste

Billington's Natural Sugars
http://wholesomesweeteners.com
Excellent light (muscovado) and
dark (molasses) brown sugar

Bob's Red Mill
www.bobsredmill.com
Graham flour, brown rice flour,
almond flour

Cabot Creamery
www.cabotcheese.coop
Excellent butter and cheddar
cheese, available in many
supermarkets

Cherry Bay Orchards
www.cherrybayorchards.com
Montmorency tart cherry
concentrate

Florida Crystals
www.floridacrystals.com
Minimally processed cane sugar

Fox's U-Bet Syrup
www.foxs-syrups.com
A variety of flavors of syrup for
egg creams, often available in
retail supermarkets

Guittard Chocolate Company
www.guittard.com
Chocolate chips, cocoa powder

Kalustyan's
http://kalustyans.com
Assorted herbs and spices, including
hard-to-find dried hibiscus flowers

King Arthur Flour
www.kingarthurflour.com
Lots of baking ingredients and
tools, including caramel color,
orange flower water, crystallized
ginger, almond flour, pistachio
paste

La Tourangelle
http://latourangelle.com
Roasted almond oil and roasted
hazelnut oil

Maple Syrup Producers
http://mainemapleproducers.com
A list of maple syrup producers
from Maine

My Brands
http://mybrands.com
Hard-to-locate and regional
brands, and some esoteric grocery
items

Nielsen-Massey Vanillas
www.nielsenmassey.com
Vanilla beans, extract, and paste

North Fork Potato Chips
www.northforkchips.com
Excellent kettle-style potato chips
made from Long Island potatoes

The Orange Shop
www.floridaorangeshop.com
Fantastic oranges and grapefruits

Pappy's
www.sassafrastea.com
Sassafras tea concentrate

Penzeys Spices
www.penzeys.com
Herbs and spices, lavender,
crystallized ginger, cocoa powder

The Redhead
http://theredheadnyc.com
Bacon Peanut Brittles

Rodelle
www.rodellekitchen.com
Vanilla beans, extract, and cocoa
powder

Rowley's Red Barn
www.southridgefarms.com
Montmorency tart cherry
concentrate

Rio Grande Organics
http://riograndeorganics.com
Certified organic pecans

Snyder's of Hanover
www.snydersofhanover.com
Old-school pretzels

Spectrum
www.spectrumorganics.com
Unrefined peanut oil

The Spice House
www.thespicehouse.com
Herbs and spices, citric acid, orange
flower water, crystallized ginger

Sprecher's Rootbeer
http://sprecherbrewery.com
Rootbeer syrup

C. S. Steen's Syrup Mill
www.steensyrup.com
Cane syrup, molasses

Tillen Farms
www.tillenfarms.com
The only maraschino cherry we'll
buy (and happily eat)

Trader Joe's
www.traderjoes.com
Lots of great ingredients, including
some rotating special in-season
fresh fruits and vegetables

The Vanilla.COMpany
http://vanilla.com
Vanilla beans, extract, and paste

Vanilla, Saffron Imports
www.saffron.com
Vanilla beans and extract

Wholesome Sweeteners
http://wholesomesweeteners.com
Minimally processed cane sugar

Wyman's of Maine
www.wymans.com
Frozen blueberries, raspberries, and
strawberries

Zulka
http://zulka.com
Minimally processed cane sugar

EQUIPMENT, SERVING WARE, AND SODA JERK ATTIRE

Amazon
www.amazon.com

Cuisinart
www.cuisinart.com
Food processors

Hamilton Beach
www.hamiltonbeach.com
Blenders

Microplane
http://us.microplane.com
Zesters and graters

Zeroll
www.zeroll.com
Ice cream scoopers

SODA FOUNTAIN MISCELLANY

American Soda Fountain, Inc.
http://americansodafountain.com
Specializes in service and repair of
soda fountains and vintage drink
dispensers

Direct2
www.direct-2u.com
Soda jerk paper hats

eBay
www.ebay.com
Soup to nuts (or in our case, seltzer
to cherry), we're always scouring
eBay for interesting fountain items,
equipment, and serving wear. After
all, we found our Bastian Blessing
soda fountain and our twirling red
barstools on eBay!

Prariemoon
www.prariemoon.biz
Everything soda fountain, from
apparel to syrups to straws

Retro Planet
www.retroplanet.com
A plethora of fun soda fountain
accessories

Soda Stream
www.sodastreamusa.com
Home soda makers, carbonators,
and other accessories

Vitamix
www.vitamix.com
High-powered blenders

Webstaurant
www.webstaurantstore.com
Fountain glasses, spoons, and plates
and an assortment of restaurant-
quality items and ingredients that
work well for the home
soda fountain

Whipped Cream Chargers
www.whippedcreamchargers.com
For everything whipped cream,
including chargers, whippers, and
soda siphons, as well as carbonated
beverage equipment

BIBLIOGRAPHY

BOOKS

Adkins, William. *The Practical Soda Fountain Guide.* St. Louis: National Druggist, 1911.

Bacon, John U. *America's Corner Store: Walgreens' Prescription for Success.* Hoboken, N.J.: John Wiley & Sons, Inc., 2004.

Binder, Frederick M., and David M. Reimers. *All the Nations Under Heaven: An Ethnic and Racial History of New York City.* New York: Columbia University Press, 1995.

Burns, Eric. *The Spirits of America: A Social History of Alcohol.* Philadelphia: Temple University Press, 2004.

Collingham, Lizzie. *The Taste of War: World War II and the Battle for Food.* New York: Penguin Press, 2012.

Davenport-Hines, Richard. *The Pursuit of Oblivion: A Global History of Narcotics.* New York: W. W. Norton & Company, Inc., 2002.

Doran, Roxana B. *Prohibition Punches: A Book of Beverages.* Philadelphia: Dorrance & Co. 1930.

Egan, Timothy. *The Worst Hard Time.* New York: Houghton Mifflin Co., 2005.

Ewen, Elizabeth. *Immigrant Women in the Land of Dollars.* New York: Monthly Review Press, 1985.

Funderburg, Anne Cooper. *Sundae Best: A History of Soda Fountains.* Bowling Green, OH: Bowling Green State University Popular Press, 2001.

Gross, Linda P., and Theresa R. Snyder. *Philadelphia's 1876 Centennial Exhibition.* Mount Pleasant, S.C.: Arcadia Publishing, 2005.

Hiss, Emile A. *The Standard Manual of Soda and Other Beverages.* Chicago: G.P. Englehard & Company, 1897.

Okrent, Daniel. *Last Call: The Rise and Fall of Prohibition.* New York: Scribner, 2010.

O'Neil, Darcy S. *Fix the Pumps.* London, Ontario: Art of Drink, 2009.

Pendergrast, Mark. *For God, Country, and Coca-Cola.* 2nd ed. New York: Basic Books, 2000.

Schloss, Andrew. *Homemade Soda.* Adams, Mass.: Storey Publishing, 2011.

Staten, Vince. *Do Pharmacists Sell Farms?: A Trip inside the Corner Drugstore.* New York: Simon & Schuster, 1998.

Welby, Adlard. *Welby's Visit to North America.* n.p. 1821.

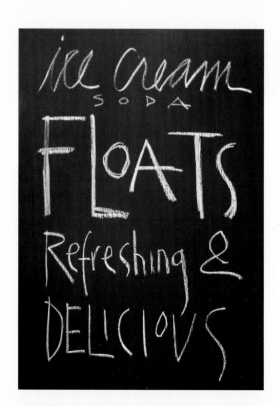

ARTICLES

Buerki, Robert A. "The Saga of Betty Brown, PhG." *Pharmacy in History* 30, no. 3 (1988): 163–167.

Coe, Andrew. "The Egg Cream Racket." *Gastronomica* 4, no. 3 (summer 2004): 18–25.

Cohen, Michael. "Jim Crow's Drug War: Race, Coca-Cola, and the Southern Origins of Drug Prohibition." *Southern Cultures* 12, no. 3 (fall 2006): 55–79.

Debus, Allen. "The Drug Store Cabaret Pharmacy and Vaudeville in 1920." *Pharmacy in History* 19, no. 1 (1977): 39–42.

Estes, J. Worth. "The Pharmacology of Nineteenth-Century Patent Medicines." *Pharmacy in History* 30, no. 1 (1988): 3–18.

Foster, Jeffrey Clayton. "A Rocky Road to a 'Drug Free Tennessee' A History of the Early Regulation of Cocaine and the Opiates, 1897–1913." *Journal of Social History* 29, no. 3 (spring 1996): 547–564.

Jackson, Richard A., and Dennis B. Worthern. "Retail Pharmacy Operations in World War II: A Profit and Loss Statement." *Pharmacy in History* 44, no. 4 (2002): 131–141.

Kremer, Steve and Mickey C. Smith. "Fibber McGee and Kremer's Drugstore." *Pharmacy in History* 59, no. 3 (2008): 119–124.

Palmer, Carl. "History of the American Soda Fountain." (1947).

Pawley, Emily. "Powerful Effervescence." *Chemical Heritage* (summer 2008).

Warner, Harry S. "Prohibition: A Step in Progress." *The ANNALS of the American Academy of Political and Social Science* 163, no. 1 (September 1932): 155–162.

Yates, Donald. "Early American Soda Fountains." *Bottles and Extras* 17 (spring 2006): 70–72.

Yates, Donald. "Tuft's Soda Fountain and Pinehurst Country Club." *Bottles and Extras* 17 (spring 2006): 2.

"Restyling Main Street for the New Deal in Beverages." *American Builder and Building Age* (1933).

TRADE JOURNALS

American Bottler (1921)

American Druggist and Pharmaceutical Record (1906–1933)

Efficient Drug Store Management (1969)

Fountain and Candy Topics (1928)

Ice Cream Trade. (1934)

Michigan Farmer (1852, vol. 10)

The Pharmaceutical Era (1895, 1908)

The Pharmacy in History (1977, 1988, 2002)

The Soda Fountain (1920–1936)

Southern Pharmaceutical Journal (1909)

The Spatula (1908–1910)

ABOUT THE TEAM

PETER FREEMAN (aka Head Jerk) is the cofounder of Brooklyn Farmacy & Soda Fountain. His degree in sociology and his love of egg creams led him to the perfect career: as a soda jerk in his own soda fountain. He lives happily above Brooklyn Farmacy & Soda Fountain with his cat, Mr. Pickles.

GIA GIASULLO (aka Big Sister) is the cofounder and creative director of Brooklyn Farmacy & Soda Fountain. She is the daughter of a Greenwich Village shopkeeper, and it is no surprise to her that after spending twenty-plus years practicing graphic design she is now runs a corner store in Brooklyn. She and her family live happily above Brooklyn Farmacy & Soda Fountain.

NELLE GRETZINGER has been involved in the day-to-day operations of the fountain since its inception. Her recipes for the Farmacy have appeared in the *New York Times* and have aired on The Cooking Channel's *Unique Sweets,* ABC's *The Chew,* and Martha Stewart Radio's *Living Today.* She lives in Brooklyn with her two daughters, both avid fans of the Farmacy.

ELIZABETH KIEM is a novelist, essayist, and literary critic. Her first novel takes place in Depression-era Coney Island and counts a soda jerk among its heroes. Her second novel, *Dancer, Daughter, Traitor, Spy,* was published in August, 2013 by Soho Teen. She is also the author of a history of Moscow and an investigative account of the international biological weapons market, which she ghost-wrote with the filmmakers Eric Nadler and Bob Coen. Elizabeth lives in Brooklyn with her husband and son not far from the Farmacy.

ERIN MERHAR is a professional chef and food stylist. Trained by the world renowned chefs of the French Culinary Institute, she worked in the heat of New York City restaurant kitchens and as a private chef in the south of France before combining her craft with her eye for detail and artistic creativity. From recipe testing and development to food styling, Erin contributes to leading U.S. food publications, cookbooks, and televisions programs. She resides in Brooklyn, just around the corner from her favorite soda fountain.

CAROLYN MORRIS (archival photographic research) is a Brooklyn based photographer. Her work has appeared in New York magazine and the Wall Street Journal. She was a participant in the Waterpod Project in New York City, and has curated several art exhibitions throughout Brooklyn.

MICHAEL HARLAN TURKELL is a once-aspiring chef and now food photographer. Based in Brooklyn, he is the former photo editor of *Edible Brooklyn* and *Edible Manhattan*, and captures the inner workings of kitchens for his James Beard Foundation nominated "Back of the House" project, which documents the working lives of chefs. He also hosts a show on HeritageRadioNetwork.org called *The Food Seen,* which touches on the intersections of food and art.

ACKNOWLEDGMENTS

We are indebted to too many "fountain angels" to ever be able to list them all, but we'll give it a whirl. Anna Van der Heide, who put up her "farm" to help jump-start our own. Bob Freeman, for imbuing us with the simple pleasure of enjoying an egg cream. Crescenzo Giasullo, who showed us what it meant to be a shopkeeper. Ezra Freeman, for his support early on in the idea. To Erez, Zoe, and Ada, who started a new life in Brooklyn so that mom could open up a soda fountain. Adam Stein, for being nothing short of an angel. Mark Stein, for being nothing short of a preservationist. Sammi Mendenhall of Mendenhall Media, Inc., for getting lost and serendipitously finding us. Charlie Fratini and the crew from Discovery Channel's *Construction Intervention*. Paul Nasrani of Adirondack Creamery, whose sweet ice cream story is intertwined with our own. Eric Demby of the Brooklyn Flea, Clinton Kelly, Marty Markowitz, Alain Ducasse, Mark Alan Stamaty, Omen A. Zen, Alan Davis, the Greenhorns, Sarah Aller, Douglas Grater, Alison Lowenstein, Rob Stupay, Morgan Berk, Lex Pelger, Julie Cohen, Teri Cunningham, Maggie Hoffman, Simmi Malhotra Degnemak, Maria Fraiser, Milton Glaser, Holley Atkinson, Slow Food NYC, Cobble Hill Variety, Kristina Hill, Pushett Irby, Claudia Ficca, Carolyn Fong, Jacob Pritchard, NYC Small Business Development Association, Jackie Newmark, Sahadis, Nine Cakes, Wilklow Orchards, Local Roots, CSA, Trois Pommes, Rio Grande Organics, Briermere Farms, The Redhead Restaurant, Roni Sue Chocolates, Rockwell Maple Farm, P&H Soda Co., Rick's Picks, Jitterbugs NYC, Brooklyn Brine Co., The Brooklyn Hot Dog Co., Flour City Pasta, Brooklyn Cured, SerendipiTea, Brooklyn Roasting Company. To the kids who celebrated when we opened and grew up before our very eyes: Henry, Zoe, Eggy, Paloma, Gabby, Thomas, Aiden, Sera, and Janelle. To our wonderful soda jerks, past and present. Our research was helped along the way by Rebecca Federman of the New York Public Library's Culinary Collections, Terry Schy from American Soda Fountain, Inc., Rabalais Books, Minnesota Historical Society, Kansas Historical Society, Sandusky Library, Norman Rockwell Museum, New York Public Library, Hastings Historical Society, National Library of Medicine, East Carolina University, Library of Congress, Oakland Museum, Oregon, University of Washington, and the State Library of Florida. To the *New York Times*, who put us on the front page of its Dining & Wine section—thanks for that! To our agent, Kari Stuart of ICM Partners, who found us on those pages and led us with grace. To Ten Speed Press, for accepting the history-food hybrid cookbook we wanted this to be. To our editors, Sara Golski and Melissa Moore, who accepted that we were so busy slinging egg creams that much of our first draft was "TK." To Sarah Adelman, for a beautifully designed book. This project was a team effort in every sense of the word and we were honored to work with Elizabeth Kiem, Nelle Gretzinger, Michael H. Turkell, Erin Merhar, and Carolyn Morris. Thank you to the fans and friends of Brooklyn Farmacy, those of you who stop in every day and those of you who travel far and wide to enjoy your first egg cream at our little fountain. To the feisty and optimistic soda fountains entrepreneurs who blazed the bubbly trail, we raise a glass of seltzer to you.

INDEX

PERMISSIONS

Page iv: Photo courtesy Jacob Pritchard; exterior, Brooklyn Farmacy & Soda Fountain.

Page vi: Photo courtesy Carolyn Fong.

Page 2: Photo courtesy Minnesota Historical Society; interior of drugstore, Fulda, MN, c. 1903.

Page 2: Image courtesy J.Y. Joyner Library Special Collections Department, East Carolina University; Mrs. Winslow's Soothing Syrup advertisement, c. 1885–6.

Page 4: Image courtesy J.Y. Joyner Library Special Collections Department, East Carolina University; Tarrant's Seltzer Aperient, c.1870–1890.

Page 5: Image courtesy National Library of Medicine, *Medicinal Mineral Waters Natural and Artificial; Their Efficacy and the Treatment of Chronic Diseases and Rules for their Employment…* S. Hanbury Smith, MD, 1856.

Page 6: Photo courtesy Minnesota Historical Society; soda fountain, MN, n.d.

Page 7: Photo courtesy Library of Congress Prints and Photographs Division; peddlers/ice drinks and snacks, 1908.

Page 8: Image courtesy J.Y. Joyner Library Special Collections Department, East Carolina University; Parkers Tonic advertisement, c.1890.

Page 8: Image courtesy J.Y. Joyner Library Special Collections Department, East Carolina University; Nichols' Bark and Iron advertisement, c. 1870–1890.

Page 9: Author's collection; formulae from *Hints to Soda Water Dispensers*, De Forest Saxe, 1898.

Page 10: Photo courtesy Oakland Museum, Oakland, Oregon, n.d.

Page 11: Photo courtesy Hastings Historical Society archives, 1909.

Page 11: Author's collection; Corbett's Rexall Store Soda Fountain ticket, 1930.

Page 12: Photo courtesy University of Washington Libraries, Special Collections Division, University of Washington; soda fountain at Shaw's Pharmacy, 1905.

Page 14: Image courtesy Rabelais, Inc., Biddeford, ME. *Descriptive Catalogue of James W. Tufts Soda Water Apparatus*; Boston: George Ellis, printer, c. 1890.

Page 15: Image courtesy Rare Books Division, The New York Public Library, Astor, Lennox, and Tilden Foundations. Agora (Restaurant), Wolf Dieter Zander Collection, n.d.

Page 16: Photo courtesy Free Library of Philadelphia/The Bridgman Art Library; James W. Tufts soda fountain, "Alhambra," 1876, American photographer.

Page 17: Author's collection; advertisements from *The Soda Fountain*, 1920.

Page 17: Author's collection; advertisements from *The Soda Fountain*, 1920.

Page 18: Photo courtesy Library of Congress; soda jerker flipping ice cream into milkshake. Corpus Christi, Texas. Photograph by Russell Lee, February, 1939.

Page 20: Image courtesy Sandusky Library Photograph Collection. Photo of Burge McNerney's ice cream wparlor, n.d.

Page 21: Image courtesy State Library and Archives of Florida Reference Collection; The Palace Soda Fountain, Tampa, Florida. c. 1925, William A. Fishbaugh Collection.

Page 22: Author's collection; advertisement from *The Soda Fountain*, 1920.

Page 24: Photo courtesy Library of Congress Prints and Photographs Division; woman seated at a soda fountain table is pouring alcohol into a cup from a cane during prohibition, February 13, 1922.

Page 26: Image courtesy J.Y. Joyner Library Special Collections Department, East Carolina University; Broadside, "Please Protect Us," c. 1908. Printed by Edwards & Broughton Printing Co., Raleigh, N.C.

Page 27: Photo courtesy Library of Congress Prints and Photographs Division; interior of a crowded bar moments before midnight, June 30, 1919 when wartime prohibition went into effect in NYC.

Page 28: Author's collection; Christo Cola advertisement from *The Soda Fountain*, 1920.

Page 31: Author's collection; Lily Cup advertisement from *The Soda Fountain*, 1920.

Page 33: Author's collection; Cover, *The Soda Fountain*, 1922.

Page 35: Image courtesy National Library of Medicine; cover of *American Druggist*, August 1929.

Page 36: Illustration © 1953 by Norman Rockwell "Soda Jerk." Printed by permission of the Norman Rockwell Family Agency. Illustration provided by Curtis Licensing. All rights reserved.

Page 38: Photo courtesy Library of Congress Prints and Photographs Division; food line during the Depression, c. 1930–40.

Page 41: Photo courtesy Minnesota Historical Society; soldier Ricky Sorenson at the soda in fountain in Anoka, after coming home, n.d.

Page 42: Illustration courtesy Milton Glaser; from "The True Origins of the Egg Cream" by Daniel Bell, *New York Magazine*, March 8, 1971.

Page 44: Photo courtesy Pushett Irby Photography, pushettirby.com; Brooklyn Farmacy & Soda Fountain staff photo, 2010.

Page 49: Photos top left and right courtesy Jacob Pritchard. Photo bottom left courtesy Kristina Hill. Photo bottom right courtesy Claudia Ficca. Brookyn Farmacy staff and guests.

Page 111: Photo courtesy Kristina Hill; Brooklyn Farmacy guests.

Page 131: Newspaper ad, *Ithaca Daily Journal*, May 28, 1892; "Platt & Colt's Sunday."

Dedicated to M. and A. Stein

Published in the United States by Ten Speed Press, an imprint of
the Crown Publishing Group, a division of Random House LLC, a
Penguin Random House Company, New York.
www.crownpublishing.com
www.tenspeed.com

Ten Speed Press and the Ten Speed Press colophon
are registered trademarks of Random House LLC

Library of Congress Cataloging-in-Publication Data
is on file with the publisher

Hardcover ISBN: 978-1-60774-484-9
eBook ISBN: 978-1-60774-485-6

Printed in China

Design by Sarah Adelman

10 9 8 7 6 5 4 3 2 1

First Edition